Reading and Writing in More Than One Language: Lessons for Teachers

Elizabeth Franklin, Editor

TESOL

Founded 1966

Teachers of English to Speakers of Other Languages, Inc.

Typeset in Sabon and Melbourne
by Capitol Communication Systems, Inc., Crofton, Maryland USA
and printed by Pantagraph Printing, Bloomington, Illinois USA

Teachers of English to Speakers of Other Languages, Inc.
1600 Cameron Street, Suite 300
Alexandria, Virginia 22314 USA
Tel 703-836-0774 • Fax 703-836-7864 • E-mail tesol@tesol.edu •
http://www.tesol.edu/

Director of Communications and Marketing: Helen Kornblum
Managing Editor: Marilyn Kupetz
Cover Design: Ann Kammerer

ISBN 0-939-791-76-5
Library of Congress Catalogue No. 98-061414

৯৯ Table of Contents

❧ Introduction

M ainstream teachers in many elementary and secondary classrooms work with students who speak languages other than
English. This book should be a valuable resource because
each chapter draws heavily on work in actual classrooms with actual
teachers, using classroom vignettes and the conversations, writings, and
artwork of bilingual students to illustrate classroom literacy practices
that help bilingual students learn to read and write effectively.

Readers of this book will

- leave it with a better idea of the language and literacy
  strengths of bilingual learners and the knowledge students
  bring to school from homes and communities

- be able to consider ways to teach literacy so that the voices of
  all the children in the classroom can be heard and so that L1
  literacy supports the development of L2 literacy

- find ways to evaluate bilingual learners so as to better understand their strengths and biliteracy development

- find ways to work with parents so that the language valued by
  the learner and community—its means, genres, and uses—is
  also present in the classroom

The contributors to this volume value the richness of literacy
practices existing in multilingual communities outside of school. To
teach bilingual students effectively to read and write, teachers need to
respect that richness their students bring from their homes. The contributors describe classrooms where the language of students—the literacy
knowledge they already possess—is respected. Students are given opportunities to read from books and materials in their primary language, to
write in their primary language, and to relate their home and community
experiences to their school experiences.

Another commonality the following chapters illustrate is the importance, as one contributor has written, of choice and voice for literacy
development. The effective bilingual teacher works on letting students

make choices about the texts they read and the texts they write and provides collaborative ways for students to talk to each other and with the teacher.

Other supportive practices in the classroom identified by the contributors include giving students the appropriate time and the space to read and write in the classroom and allowing for the use of many different symbol systems—art or conversation, for example, rather than only reading and writing. The effective teacher also needs to be able to notice and document what students are doing in the classroom regarding their literacy development. Teachers who can notice and think about students' writing, art, conversation, and reading over a period of time will discover their own resources appropriate for each child.

The following chapters move from rich and helpful descriptions of a wide variety of bilingual literacy activities across various grade levels (Freeman & Freeman; Urzúa; Samway & Syvanen) to the description of an individual classroom and practice (Weed & Ford) to the study and description of individual bilingual children (Hudelson; Franklin; Maguire), and we hope that these differences will allow different readers points of entry into the issues involved. However, each chapter ends in the same way: with a list of suggestions for classroom practice that we believe teachers will find helpful.

Hoping for "School Success for Secondary English Learners," Yvonne and David Freeman present some of the challenges that secondary English learners face, including problems with assessment and placement that can render them invisible, unavailable for attention or appropriate instruction. The Freemans blend theory with practice to provide the secondary teacher with sound and useful ideas. They show how Cortés's four-level model of multiculturation (mainstream empowerment, intergroup understanding, group resource, and civic commitment) can be used as goals for teachers, and they also present teachers helping students achieve these goals, showing student work that illustrates that development.

Carole Urzúa looks at "The Everyday Surprise: Nourishing Literacy in the Classroom" and describes strong classroom literacy environments. Literacy, Urzúa demonstrates, grows in purposeful settings where students make choices among a diversity of materials and activities. It also grows—and her example of Vuong, a Cambodian sixth-grade student, is important—as a series of literate behaviors, not literacy skills, and it grows best in authentic environments where the literacies of home and school are integrated.

In "Cross-Age Tutoring and ESOL Students," Katharine Davies Samway and Carlyn Syvanen report on their study of the process of older second language students tutoring younger ones—they find it an effective practice. The younger students were helped by having access to a fellow speaker, listening to and using English in a relatively stress-free context. The older students gained as well, not only by practicing authentic encounters with English print but by being allowed to be experts, something they rarely experienced in mainstream classrooms.

Studying one particular classroom, Kathryn Weed and Monica Ford suggest ways of "Achieving Literacy Through Multiple Meaning Systems," by examining a richly diverse, multigrade, multilingual situation. Monica, the classroom teacher, uses a variety of expressive and communicative modes—listening, discussing, sketching, writing, music, drama, and movement—as ways of helping students conceptualize their experience and come to deeper understandings. Freed from initial concerns— mechanics, for example—the children are able to experience reading and writing as a seamless whole and, as they experience the various symbol systems, they see their own strengths as artists, authors, and presenters of information.

Sarah Hudelson ("Evaluating Reading, Valuing the Reader") focuses on an individual child—Juanita—from first to third grade, documenting her development and indicating a "complete, complex, and detailed" view of Juanita's use of English and Spanish. This study, including observations of book responses, oral reading, independent reading, writings, notes from conversations and literature responses in both languages, shows how important it is to bring assessment of children's learning more in line with the actual teaching being done.

My own chapter on "The Fiction Writing of Two Dakota Boys" focuses on Richard and Jonathan making choices in a classroom that emphasized both student knowledge and interest and teacher input in developing curricula for individual children. Because writing is both personally expressive and culturally situated at the same time, a report on a study of these two students' writing shows their individual preferences and their cultural influences as expressed in their choices of subject matter, genre, and style.

The last chapter, Mary Maguire's "A Bilingual Child's Choices and Voices: Lessons Noticing, Listening, and Understanding," reflects on 4 years of a child's life in a striking literacy situation. Heddie is involved in two mainstream languages at school (English and French) and two nonmainstream languages at home (Persian and Arabic). Maguire shows how these languages function for Heddie, who, aware of moving within a variety of family, school, and cultural discourses, questions and articulates her emerging self. Maguire's study shows the richness and tensions of literacy development and how social, cultural, historical, and political forces come together in forming an individual identity.

These are large issues, all of them, and I believe this book will help professional educators address the important social and cultural ramifications of our work with children. In this book, you will be able to hear the voices of individual teachers and educators as they work with students, documenting and reflecting on the personal meanings they find in classroom practice. And, perhaps, most importantly, this book also echoes with the voices of young people such as Juanita, Heddie, Richard, Felipe, and Vuong—voices you will want to hear and understand, just as you hear and understand them in your own classrooms, day after day.

BETH FRANKLIN
University of Nebraska–Lincoln

Chapter ✍ 1

School Success for Secondary English Learners

Yvonne Freeman and David Freeman

Mi nombre es Noé soy estudiante de Jefferson High School, y mi interes es estudiar mucho para poder ser algien en la vida y asi tener un futuro bueno para mi y mi familia.

[My name is Noé. I am a student at Jefferson High School and my interest is to study a lot in order to be able to be someone in life and thus to have a good future for me and my family.]

In his statement, Noé reflects the hopes and dreams that many students feel as they enter our schools. Noé wants to "be someone" and to have a good future "for me and my family." He writes about his hopes and dreams in Spanish because he is a recent immigrant from Mexico. His parents came to this country several years ago, leaving their children in the care of an aunt. As soon as the parents had steady jobs, they sent money for Noé and his younger sister to come. Now Noé is studying so he can obtain a good job and help his family develop their dreams for a better life.

Noé attended a small country school in Mexico, where he received a somewhat limited education. Noé expresses himself here in Spanish because he knows that his teacher, George, can read Spanish and supports the use of his students' L1. Noé's Spanish lacks spelling and punctuation conventions, but it communicates an important message to his teacher.

George teaches math at a large, urban high school with many students like Noé who are just learning English. As part of a college class in language acquisition, George conducted a case study on Noé. George understood the importance of literacy development for the academic

1

success of English learners (Cummins, 1994; Freeman & Freeman, 1994, 1997; Krashen, 1985). Despite the fact that he was teaching math, George knew that Noé needed to develop literacy in English as well as in Spanish to succeed in school. He was especially concerned about Noé's English reading. He noticed that Noé appeared to "read very well" and that his ESL teachers liked him "because they have reading groups in their ESL classes, and this guy can zoom along just like any other kid." However, what George discovered was that Noé was just decoding the English. When George asked Noé to read a word problem aloud and then tell what the problem meant, "he had no idea."

When George recognized the difference between Noé's apparent proficiency in oral reading and his actual level of understanding, he was able to begin designing lessons to help Noé do the academic reading he needed to succeed in school and get the kind of job that would help him realize his dreams. For one thing, George helped his students focus on key words. He explained in his case study how he had students identify and discuss important terms in word problems: "for example, key words for subtraction would be *diminished by*, *difference*, or *descend*." George's lessons helped his students develop the academic language they needed to succeed in school.

Noé is fortunate. He has a sensitive teacher who supports his L1 and who values his primary culture. He has parents who provide a stable, financially secure home and reinforce the idea that education is the way to success. He has developed basic literacy in Spanish and has studied academic subjects in his L1.

ஐ Challenges for English Learners and Their Teachers

Noé's situation is a positive one in many respects. However, there are also many challenges Noé and many other secondary school English learners face. Each year the number of students like Noé who enter U.S. schools with limited English proficiency increases. In the district where George teaches nearly one third of the students (25,089 of 78,000) were classified as LEP in 1996, and about 25% of the LEP students were high school age. This district is not unusual. In California, more than 1.3 million students were classified LEP in 1996.

Because L1 support is seldom available in secondary schools, Noé and most students like him are placed in a total English program. That means their academic development will necessarily be delayed while they are learning English. Research by Thomas and Collier (1995) has shown that even when immigrant students have had schooling in their L1 and begin schooling here in Grade 7, they have a difficult time reaching the

50th percentile on standardized tests given in English in the academic content areas by Grade 12. In fact, the Thomas and Collier study showed that students taught ESL traditionally in classes emphasizing language structure barely made it to the 25th percentile by Grade 12. In contrast, those secondary students in classes using more current methods for teaching English through academic content did somewhat better, reaching the 34th or 40th percentile on standardized tests by Grade 12.

Clearly, for students like Noé and teachers like George to succeed, a number of obstacles must be overcome. In the sections that follow, we analyze three challenges facing English learners and their teachers. First, many students like Noé are placed in classes that are not appropriate for them. Second, once in a class, particularly if they are not discipline problems, such students may not receive much attention. In a sense, they become invisible. Third, many of these students exit from high school without fully developed academic literacy in their first or second languages and with limited academic content knowledge.

After discussing these challenges, we consider what the goals of an effective program should be. We present Cortés' (1994) model of multiculturation as a way of working effectively with secondary English learners, helping them to acculturate rather than assimilate as they learn to succeed academically. We explain the goals of multiculturation and show how they might be implemented in secondary classrooms. Throughout the chapter we offer examples of how teachers like George have used reading and writing activities with secondary students to help move them toward academic success.

Challenges From Assessment, Placement, and Appropriate Instruction

One of the first challenges schools face is how to assess and place students like Noé who often arrive without detailed records of past schooling. Teachers like George seldom have access to information about past coursework in specific subject areas such as math. Schools are required to assess students' language proficiency, but some schools lack personnel to provide adequate primary language assessment. For example, in Fresno, California, where we work, students in the local school district speak more than 100 different home languages.

Even testing for English proficiency can be problematic. Often, the tests only assess oral language, but students' academic success depends crucially on their ability to read and write. Many students with good oral English skills lack the academic literacy needed to do well in school. Cummins (1981) has pointed out the important difference between conversational and academic language. If students can speak and understand English in informal settings, teachers may assume that the students are fully proficient, and these students may be mainstreamed even though they have not developed the academic language they need for content area classes.

Collier (1995) argues that language development, cognitive development, and academic development are closely interrelated. All three areas also affect a student's social and cultural development. What makes appropriate placement difficult, then, is that a number of factors affect the academic achievement of second language students.

Victoria, a junior high girl from rural Mexico, is a good example of the challenges involved in appropriate assessment and placement. Unlike Noé, Victoria is from a large family. Her father returned to Mexico several years ago. Her mother is taking care of eight other children and does not want Victoria to stay with her, so she lives with her grandmother. Victoria's grandmother has many problems of her own to cope with and does not understand the U.S. school system. As a result, no one in Victoria's family has interceded as an advocate for her in her academic placement.

When she was in elementary school, Victoria was shuttled between Mexican and U.S. schools and did not develop strong literacy skills in either Spanish or English. By Grade 6, she was placed in a special education class because she was several grade levels behind her peers as measured by standardized tests. She was diagnosed as having language delay and received additional help from a speech therapist. It was recommended that she be taught completely in English because earlier sporadic instruction in Spanish had not produced the desired result.

Despite that recommendation, the next year Victoria was mainstreamed from a special education class into a class where she continued to receive some special education services as well as support in her primary language. At the end of only a year her IQ score had risen by 16 points on a standardized IQ test.

Victoria is now in Grade 9. Mary, a speech and language specialist began working with Victoria recently. She immediately noted how a variety of inappropriate tests have been used to measure Victoria's language and academic abilities at different stages of her schooling, and how the result has been an inconsistent educational program. In fact, when Mary pointed out her concerns about Victoria and her suspicion that Victoria was misdiagnosed and misplaced from her initial assessment, her present bilingual junior high teacher said, "Oh, she was. She didn't ever belong in special education." Mary is determined to see to it that Victoria is taken out of the special education program, but Victoria is about to enter a high school where no bilingual support is available. Her home life is unstable. Her outlook for academic success is not bright.

Challenges From Students Who Become Invisible

A more subtle challenge, but nevertheless an important one, is posed by students who face serious academic difficulties but who seem to become invisible to their teachers. These are the students who do not cause any problems but do not do very well either. They seem to disappear inside the school system, and if they do make their way through the system, they often emerge without the academic knowledge and skills they really need. These invisible students pose a second challenge to schools.

Both Noé and Victoria were fortunate. They were given special attention by their teachers and support personnel. George encouraged Noé to write in Spanish and spent extra time talking with him. He also changed the way he taught math so that he could meet the needs of his second language students. George was doing an excellent job. Unfortunately, when a problem arose in an algebra class at his school, parents of the algebra students petitioned that George be transferred to teach that class (where there were no language minority students), and his math students were split up and put into other classes. Thus, Noé lost an important source of support due to an administrative decision. Victoria has recently been given bilingual support and the special services of Mary, but there is no guarantee that an appropriate program will be available for her in high school. Often, English learners do not even get the kind of attention that Noé and Victoria received.

Chi, a Hmong student just entering junior high, is probably more typical. Shelly, her junior high ESL teacher, describes Chi as having had "a long, hard struggle with understanding and learning English." When Chi entered Shelly's class, her English was so limited that Shelly thought she was a recent arrival and was surprised to find "it was already her third year." Like other English learners, Chi "had been sitting patiently, waiting for someone to teach her something." Shelly noted, "She is very shy and quiet, so she has not taken many risks and has very few verbal skills." Secondary teachers have many students each day, and if students are quiet and well behaved, they may escape the teachers' notice. The result is that these students do not develop either the English language proficiency or the academic knowledge they need to succeed.

At least Chi has been in the same school district for 3 years. Migrant students face additional problems. Rubén, who teaches English in a rural high school, comments that many of his students "feel they are outsiders wherever they go. Some come to school for short periods of time— knowing they will soon be moving again." When students move frequently, it is particularly difficult for schools to keep accurate records of their academic progress. In addition, migrant students may lose motivation. As Rubén says, "I can almost always pick out these students by their lack of interest. They don't seem to feel like trying and do not attempt to make many friends." Rubén works hard to involve his migrant students, to respect them, and to make them feel "not so invisible," but his job is extremely difficult, and the chances for success for these students are not high.

Some students with a stable home life and strong home support still struggle simply because they are English learners. Denise described her student, Miguel, as "a well-behaved boy who was well liked by other students. He was a nicely dressed, well-groomed, polite child—the kind most teachers find very easy to like." Miguel 's father was "Always dressed in suit and tie." He wanted his son to do well in school, and he insisted that Denise give Miguel plenty of homework. Even though Miguel's mother spoke no English, his father did not want the son to read and write in Spanish and did not encourage his primary language development at home.

Miguel did very well in Denise's class, both academically and socially, so Denise assumed that he had a high level of academic English proficiency. However, one day she realized that Miguel had developed strategies to cloak his lack of English. As Denise put it, "He was very clever at hiding his misunderstandings, however, so it was several months into the school year before I discovered this." What triggered Denise's realization was an assignment she made. "I had given a series of verbal instructions to the whole class. The assignment of tasks was somewhat more abstract than I usually gave." As other students began work, Denise noticed that Miguel was just sitting at his desk "doing nothing." At first Denise thought her student was experiencing some personal problems. It was only after she asked him directly, "Tell me what you are thinking," that he revealed that he had no idea what to do. Denise commented, "It was then that I realized the decontexualized nature of my assignment simply wasn't comprehensible to him." Good teacher that she is, Denise made sure to contextualize future instructions and to observe Miguel more carefully to confirm that he understood assignments.

Miguel was not invisible in the same way that Rubén and Shelly's students were, but his lack of proficiency was invisible to his teacher for several months. Denise, at least, was sensitive to her student and made the needed adjustment. Kellie, a secondary teacher education candidate, observed a class taught by another student teacher who lacked that sensitivity. Kellie explained how this world history teacher "gave the class an assignment from the textbook and then told them not to talk to one another, just complete their work." Kellie further wrote that "He then came over and told me that one of his students could not read." Kellie was amazed that the teacher would make this kind of assignment knowing that at least one student who could not read could not even begin to complete it. He further kept students from possibly helping each other make sense of the assignment by prohibiting any talking. It was as though that student (and probably others as well) just did not count.

Fortunately, most secondary teachers do work hard to help students succeed under difficult circumstances. Melissa, for instance, deals with many students in her high school English classes who seem to have given up and are just putting in their time. They may recognize that their academic and language proficiencies are not adequate to the demands of some classes. Melissa refuses to accept this acceptance of failure. As she puts it, "What this means for me, though, as a teacher is that I have to be willing to work harder. If one expects failure, that's what one gets." Although some teachers, like the one Kellie observed, simply do not have the experience or resources needed to meet the needs of all their students, others like Melissa do. However, all too often English learners simply become invisible to some of their teachers.

Challenges From Students Who Develop Only Partial Linguistic and Academic Development

Even when English learners are able to graduate from high school, they still may not have developed the academic and linguistic abilities or the confidence they need to continue their education. Wanda, who teaches at a community college, described Carlos, a 19-year-old freshman:

> Carlos arrived in the United States when he was 13-years-old. He came from a city in the Philippines and spoke Tagalog. Carlos was fortunate enough to come from a wealthy background that allowed him to attend private schools in his native country. His parents held professional jobs in the Philippines but felt a move to the United States would give their son more opportunities . . . . Carlos's parents always stressed the importance of a good education and introduced Carlos to the English language before he came to the United States. All of these aspects of parental support, an education from his native country, and a positive self-image from coming from the upper classes within his society lend themselves to predict a certain degree of success in school.

Even with all these advantages, however, Carlos had trouble adjusting. He arrived for Grade 7, "a year of difficult transition even for many American students." He was isolated and had trouble making friends because of his ethnic background. He received extra support in high school, but still his grades were low. Wanda noted that "Carlos was determined to graduate and took summer school courses and worked twice as hard during the school term." He was able to graduate, but then he was placed in a remedial English course in community college. He was the only nonnative speaker in Wanda's class. He sat apart from the other students and confided to Wanda that "speaking in front of a large group was his worst nightmare." He was afraid other students would ridicule him because of his English.

Carlos struggled in Wanda's class. He had taken on a part-time job and simply did not seem to have the extra energy he needed to concentrate on his school assignments. Although he had made it into college, his chances of success at that level were not good. Carlos seems typical of those English learners who complete the requirements for secondary schools but are not adequately prepared for higher education.

A further example comes from Linda, who teaches freshman composition at a small liberal arts college. Carolina, one of Linda's students, did not have the advantages Carlos had. Carolina's family came to the United States from Mexico when she was 7. The eldest of six children, Carolina is the first of her family to attend college. However, her self-esteem and her literacy skills are both low. Carolina writes:

> I don't consider myself a good reader or writter. I always have trouble starting a writting assignment. I know about what I want to write, I have ideas, but I can't find the right way to get started. As a reader I don't think I'm good either specially at something I'm not interested in. If its something I don't like I'll have a hard time understanding.

Even though Carolina says she hopes "to improve alot my reading and writting," one wonders if she is ready for the difficult classes she will be attending. Like Carlos, she has been placed in a special writing class. We hope that both Carlos and Carolina will succeed, but we are concerned that they are starting college with many obstacles still to overcome. They have come further than Noé, Victoria, and the other secondary students we described earlier, but they still face serious challenges, and so do their teachers.

❧ The Goal for Teachers of Learners of English: Multiculturation

We have been focusing on the challenges that English learners and their teachers face. Many second language learners at the secondary level lack full academic, cognitive, and language development. Often, these students have been assessed incorrectly and have not received the kind of instruction that would have helped them the most. Some have had teachers who have not been sensitive to their needs. Many have simply been invisible, passing quietly through the system without ever really learning very much.

Even though these problems quite clearly exist, many teachers are finding ways to succeed with all their students. They are engaging their English learners in meaningful reading and writing rather than silencing them. They are working to help students build the self-esteem they need for high levels of academic, cognitive, and language development.

Like all students, English learners have many different needs. The question, then, becomes "What are appropriate goals for teachers working with second language students?" Teachers are concerned with helping students develop academic, cognitive, and language proficiency, but to what end? That is, if we teach all students to read and write, what should they be learning in this process?

Cortés (1994) suggests that the goal should be what he calls *multiculturation*. According to Cortés, multiculturation is "a convenient blending of 'multiple' and 'acculturation'" (p. 24). He uses the term *acculturation* rather than *assimilation*. As he explains it, "acculturation means learning to adapt to mainstream culture while assimilation means attempting to adopt it as yours" (p. 26). Cortés points out that acculturation is additive, but assimilation is often subtractive. Many language minority students lose their primary language and culture without ever being able to fully adopt mainstream culture. They end up with less, not more.

Jasmine Alvarez's (1995) piece (see p. 10) comes from *Voices of Reflection*, a 1995 publication from Diana Cáliz's high school American, European, and ethnic literature classes. Diana teaches in a large San Francisco high school and describes her students and their yearly publication:

> The work reflects the thoughts of sophomore, junior, and senior students in regular English classes. Many of these students are still learning English and may be in one ESL class during the day. Some are native born students; but they are all asked to consider the issues facing our multicultural society. They write with honesty and conviction. (Personal communication)

Jasmine's words in "Who Am I?" reflect the honesty and conviction Diana mentions. She "takes pride in her culturally enriched blood." She loves her family, her culture, and her native language, but she also sees herself as part of "generations of dreams, of all those Salvadorian people who wanted to (be) born in the United States for a chance at a better life." Jasmine sees herself as a contributing part of the larger society: "I am a helper of my community, and a hard worker." She is an example of a student who has acculturated rather than being assimilated. She has adapted to mainstream society without losing her primary culture.

In the same publication, Amy Chan (1995), a student in Diana's

Jasmine Alvarez
American Lit. 1

Who am I?

When I hear the question , "Who are you?", at times it makes me wonder , but this is what I believe I am and represent .

I see myself as a Salvadorian of European and Mayan descendance. I am a person who takes pride in her culturally enriched blood which flows through my body.

I am a helper of my community , and a hard worker. I am a dedicated Roman Catholic, with a good heart and good values.

I am a loving daughter ,sister, and girlfriend. I am a good friend to lean on and someone whose easy to talk to.

I am that person who loves her family, her culture, it's customs, and my Native tongue. I am generations of dreams, of all those Salvadorian people who wanted to born in the United States for a chance at a better life.

All in all, I am Jasmine Elizabeth Alvarez, the result of generations of love, hopes, and dreams. I am a proud Latina whose family has overcome many obstacles and who has many more obstacles to confront.

Jasmine E. Alvarez c/o 1996

FIGURE 1.

European literature class, also reflected an acculturation rather than an assimilation approach to her life in the United States in her response to Amy Tan's (1993) essay, "Mother Tongue":

> "Mother Tongue" is my favorite essay. As a child of Chinese immigrant parents, I can see many likenesses with Amy Tan. The attitudes of learning English as a second language and the feeling toward her mother's 'limited' English Tan talks about in "Mother Tongue" are very true . . . . Like Amy Tan, I also like language. Although learning a language is not easy, I believe I will gain much happiness once I can

master English . . . . I think it will not take too long for me to master English. My aunt always brags, 'My daughter has forgotten Chinese now. It has been only three years since she has come here. She speaks English now.' I don't understand how a person can so easily forget their native language, which has been used for more than fifteen years, within three years. I want to master English, but I want to master Chinese too. As Amy Tan explained, "It's my mother tongue." (pp. 66–68)

These literature reflections show that Diana's students are becoming acculturated rather than assimilated. The study of appropriate literature assists them in this process (see Multicultural Literature Suggestions for Adolescents at the end of this chapter). The students have a sense of pride in their cultural heritage, a desire to maintain their native language, and a determination to both achieve in and contribute to the mainstream society. Diana and other teachers have found an approach to reading and writing that helps their students move toward multiculturation.

Cortés (1994) identifies four kinds of acculturation that can serve as goals for English learners and their teachers. The four elements of the multiculturation model are

1. mainstream empowerment acculturation: the development of the ability to function effectively as part of the mainstream

2. intergroup understanding acculturation: the development of "intercultural knowledge, understanding, and sensitivity in an increasingly racially, ethnically, culturally, and linguistically diverse society" (p. 25)

3. group resource acculturation: the development of the different resources of students who come from diverse backgrounds

4. civic commitment acculturation: the development of a sense of "concern for and commitment to others and willingness to act on the basis of that caring in order to work toward a more just, equitable society" (p. 25)

In the following sections, we offer examples of secondary teachers helping students toward the goals of multiculturation. We recognize that any one classroom activity or assignment may meet more than one of these goals simultaneously, but we have organized the examples by goal and focused on ways that teachers have met each goal.

ঙ Goal 1: Mainstream Empowerment Acculturation

The first kind of acculturation Cortés identifies is mainstream empower-ment acculturation. It is often difficult to help English learners "function effectively as part of the mainstream" without also forcing assimilation on them. It is not easy for secondary teachers to accomplish what Diana has done with her students. Community and school attitudes make it hard for teachers to empower their students to acculturate rather than assimilate. However, an increasing number of secondary teachers are doing just that.

Ron, a teacher in a large, rural high school with a high Hispanic population, describes his setting:

> The high school where I teach has an assimilation philosophy. That attitude is reflected in the way English is taught. At the high school level the emphasis is on the preparation of students for college and career. Most students will need strong English language skills to be successful. Teachers feel their task is to help students fit into the college and career systems as they are now in the United States.

Students do need to develop the skills and build the background that allows them to succeed in the mainstream. If they can do that and also maintain their primary language and culture, they can avoid assimila-tion. Although Ron refers to his school as *assimilationist*, his own practices reveal that Ron's real goal for his students is acculturation. When he started to study about second language issues, Ron commented, "although I celebrate and help students learn about other cultures and languages, my job is to prepare them for what is immediately ahead." He is definitely trying to help his students to develop "the ability to function effectively as part of the mainstream." Because of his studies, Ron is also coming to value the other part of an acculturation stance and is recognizing how important it is to "celebrate and help students learn about other cultures and languages" including the students' own.

Ron has recently begun to expand the kinds of literature his students read. The impetus for this change came from an ESL methods class Ron took. Students in the graduate class engaged in a literature study. They could choose among novels about adolescents from different cultural backgrounds. Ron chose to read *Shabanu* (Fisher-Staples, 1989), a novel about a Pakistani teenager whose parents have arranged her marriage. Shabanu loves the camels she and her nomadic family herd, but her parents want her to move into a city. Ron felt that his students could relate to Shabanu despite the cultural differences between his students and this Pakistani girl. In his literature reflection, Ron wrote, "*Shabanu* opened up a new world for me, and that is the major mark of a good novel. A novel, according to Bahktin (in Wertsch, 1991), is characterized by openness. It is not a closed system; it creates characters and situations and makes them come alive by imparting to them the quality of openness that we feel in human existence." Although *Shabanu* is not on most lists for developing cultural literacy, it has the qualities of good literature, and Ron saw that he could use it to help his students develop needed literary knowledge.

Ron appreciated the kind of literature study he experienced in his graduate course. "The literature study we did, in the style of the grand conversation method (Peterson & Eeds, 1990), allowed us to maintain and explore the openness in the novel." Later, in his own classroom, Ron used this approach with his students. As Ron noted, "This type of literature study is what adolescents need. At their developmental stage they are wrestling with identity issues. To close down this exploration in the classroom by denying them an approach to the varied dialogues within a novel and about a novel denies them material with which they can develop identity."

For mainstream empowerment acculturation to occur, both the approach to studying literature in the classroom and the literature itself are important. Ron has begun to expand his students' choices.

Rather than only reading traditional literature such as *Don Quixote*, which really does not reflect the Mexican and Latin American heritage of his students, Ron has begun doing choice literature studies. He recently purchased sets of novels about teens from a variety of cultural background struggling to understand their world (e.g., *Shabanu*), and he uses these novels now in his classroom.

Often secondary teachers are not aware of the rich resources available for literature studies. Chrissy, a new teacher, who was also in Ron's ESL methods class, chose *Shadow of the Dragon* (Garland, 1993) for her literature study. She immediately recognized how she could use this adolescent novel: "This was a powerful book and I think it would stimulate a lot of thought in a classroom literature study." Chrissy identified four possible directions she could take with this novel. First, she felt it would help dispel misconceptions about Southeast Asians. "The focus on this aspect could lead to discussions about misconceptions about others, about the difficulties when entering the new country, and the stereotyping of ethnic groups." Second, the novel deals with the dilemmas ESL students face and their classroom realities. This too could lead to important discussions. Third, "The title of the book was derived from a Vietnamese folk tale. This focus could lead to a lesson on folk tales, the importance of stories and story telling in particular cultures, and the use of tales to explain changes in life." The fourth direction Chrissy identified was "The search and the journey for self-discovery," another universal literary theme. Using a literature study format with novels about adolescents from different cultures allows teachers like Chrissy and Ron to provide their second language students with the literary skills they need to succeed in mainstream classes and the opportunity to reflect on and value their diverse cultural heritages.

A different example of mainstream empowerment acculturation comes from Loretta's junior high school English and social studies ESL classes. Loretta, who has a background in business education as well as a master's degree in language development, wanted her students to have an authentic purpose for reading and writing English. At the same time, she wanted them to begin to think about the many possibilities they have in their futures. Loretta recruited volunteer adults from a manufacturing firm, an insurance company, and a hospital to begin a pen pal exchange with her students. Many of these adults were from different minority groups. After several months of exchanging letters, the pen pals met. Students and adults talked to together, and the students also gave their pen pals a book the class had created. On each page was a computer-generated picture of one of the students and a sample of that student's writing. The students read their page to their pen pal. Nou Vang wrote the following poem for the book:

Nou

Sleep, lazy, funny, and kind
son of Shoua and Va Lor Vang
lover of cousins, parents and girlfriend
Who feels nice, happy and wonderful
Who finds happiness, love and family
Who needs love and understanding
Who gives gifts, happiness and love
Who fears being laugh at, bad thing and being talk about.
Who would like to see past, future and Laos
Who enjoys playing with friends, games and sports
Who likes to wear blue, black and green
Resident of Clovis. (p. 38)

The local newspaper covered the meeting of the students and adults, which turned out to be extremely successful for both groups. Fourteen-year-old María, who arrived recently from the Philippines, met with Jeaninne, a human resources assistant for the manufacturing firm. In describing María, Jeaninne explained that she and María had common interests: "We both like math . . . . She realized after talking to me that you use math after getting out of school" (p. B2, Reddin, 1995). María explained, "I learned so much . . . about the business world, how important it is to get a college degree." Another student, Javier, explained that he learned "that you have to go by a certain dress code and you can't be late for work because it could cost you your job" (p. B2, Reddin, 1995).

These basic concepts are critical for junior high school students to learn at this early age. During the meeting, Loretta had her students read to the adults in both English and their primary languages because she wants to enhance their bilingualism. The principal of Loretta's school spoke to the group and emphasized that the English learners in this project were part of the regular academic program. He commented, "We're not watering down the curriculum." He also noted that "the diversity of students in the class brings a real enhancement to both English and social studies lessons." When school administrators express this type of philosophy and teachers support it with projects such as this one, they are encouraging their students toward mainstream empowerment acculturation.

❧ Goal 2: Intergroup Understanding Acculturation

The second element of Cortés's (1994) acculturation model is intergroup understanding acculturation, which is the development of "intercultural knowledge, understanding, and sensitivity in an increasingly racially, ethnically, culturally, and linguistically diverse society" (p. 25). Diana's high school literature students work on this type of understanding throughout the year as they read, discuss, and write about powerful pieces of literature. Monica Liang (1994) explains this well (see Figure 2).

In Diana's class, students of different races and cultures study about each other and write their impressions. After reading several articles about slavery, Liang wrote a piece entitled "To Be a Slave" in *American Mosaic*. In her writing she expressed her indignation at the way slaves were treated:

> I read such sad things as a mother who killed her own baby because she didn't want the baby to be taken away from her and to be sold to others. This actually happened! It was just too sad and terrible that I couldn't find a word to describe my feelings! (p. 15)

She concluded her essay by describing the bravery of another slave woman, writing, "I was just simply stunned by her strength and courage. I admired her. Great going, warrior!"

Rowena Reyes (1994) wrote a poem about African Americans entitled, "A Proud People" (see Figure 3) in which she shows not only

---

American Mosaic

"American Mosaic" is inlaid with pieces of students' feelings and opinions toward America's different faces: slavery and freedom; peace and war; poverty and wealth. Students also expressed their thoughts on the themes of freedom, racism, tolerance, violence, friendship, family value, war, cultural diversity, prejudice, beauty, and much more.

Through the students' creative writings, poems, response journals, essays, visuals, and drawings, you can share their unique feelings and the impressions of America. The persistent efforts of the students in Ms. Caliz's American Literature and Ethnic Literature classes have created this beautiful "American Mosaic."

BY: Monica Liang

Monica Liang

FIGURE 2.

sympathy for the injustices of slavery and an understanding of history but also a knowledge of the heroes and writers who try to express the importance of cultural pride and understanding. It is important for students to understand and appreciate their own cultures, but when students from different cultural groups study about and learn to appreciate the beauty of all groups, they are moving toward an intercultural understanding that leads to hope.

Shelly, a middle school ESL teacher, used a popular piece of literature and food to get her students to begin to appreciate each other's cultures. Shelly began by using both the Spanish and English versions of the literature book, *Everybody Cooks Rice* (Dooley, 1991, 1993). In this book, the main characters move from house to house in their neighborhood where different neighbors from different ethnic groups are preparing different rice dishes. The book includes recipes for each of the rice dishes. Shelly explained her rationale for using the book:

> Exploring the fact that many cultures eat rice and examining their recipes allows students to see that although a rice dish tastes or looks different, the basic ingredient, rice, is the same (even the different kinds

A Proud People   by   Rowena Reyes   5°

Black History Month—
What is Black History Month?
Is it just another holiday?
Is it just another someday?
Or is it an awareness?
of proud people.

Black History—
a proud people
Not slaves
not just maids.
Not for whites,
who deprived them
of their rights.
A proud people

A building of a railroad,
didn't just unite our road,
but a road of proud people

They fought in the Civil War
to open a closed door;
a door of shattered dreams
and for a war of deprived people
Truly a proud people

Martin Luther King,
held the wings to great change.
A proud people
Langston Hughes,
not just a show it,
but a justified poet.
A proud people
Frederick Douglass,
a writer and not a fighter.
A proud people
Yes, a proud people.

Close to independence,
they stuck to their amendments,
an amendment of equality
for proud people

July 4th,
a day for proud people
They gained their independence
from a road of deprived dreams,
dreams that were not true,
are now accessible to me and you.
What a proud people !
What really a proud people !

FIGURE 3.

of rice are still rice!). Through discussion, the students can make the analogy that although people may look different or speak a different language, they are still the same inside; they have the same ingredients. This helps to foster understanding and create a sense of commonalty between students.

To teach the lesson, Shelly began by reading the book and encouraging general class discussion. Then she divided the class into seven groups. She had precooked rice and had most of the other ingredients ready for students in the groups to prepare each of the seven rice dishes. Students then tasted each dish and wrote descriptions of each rice dish on large pieces of butcher paper posted on the wall near each dish. Of course, more class discussion followed this activity. Shelly suggests several extensions for this lesson:

Different groups in the class can choose one of the families in the story, research their cultural heritage and give a class presentation. Also, if the culture of a student in the class is not represented in the book, that student may create an additional section, explaining his or her rice recipe. Other common foods may also be explored and a class book could be generated. For example, pig's feet are common to Mexican, African American, and Hmong recipes.

Through reading, writing, and hands on activities, teachers can help students move toward intergroup understandings that will help them see the values in the backgrounds of their peers. That appreciation leads to Cortés's third kind of acculturation, group resource acculturation.

ða Goal 3: Group Resource Acculturation

Cortés (1994) explains that in a multicultural society it is necessary "to provide the best education for all, while at the same time recognizing the existence of individual and group differences that influence the process of attaining that education" (p. 30). He goes on to explain that educators must find ways to contribute to building on cultural differences in a way that "both increases individual opportunities and adds to the richness of U.S. society." Education for English learners must serve authentic purposes, with students "learning to read, write, speak, and hear the language and not just translate printed passages and take grammar examinations" (p. 30). Finally, Cortés explains that the home languages of English learners must be seen as a valuable resource that "can enhance individual and career opportunities and help students become more effective contributing citizens in a nation and world in which bilingual and multicultural skills will be both personal and societal assets" (p. 32).

Teachers who develop group resources find innovative ways to help English learners value themselves, their cultures, and their languages, and, at the same time, help mainstream students appreciate the diversity around them. Kathy, a high school Spanish teacher, and Carol, the ESL teacher at the same school, have been concerned about enabling their European American and Hispanic students to see the benefits of working together. They decided to have their classes meet together every other week so that students would have the opportunity to practice their new language with peers. Kathy explained the procedure:

> Carol and I alternate languages. For example, the last time we met, we instructed the students to speak only Spanish and to only use English if there was a real need. The idea is to inspire in the students the confidence to talk and to use whatever elements of the language that

would help them to communicate effectively. Both the ESL and the Spanish students are very cooperative and try hard to stick to the format.

Carol felt that her beginning-level ESL students, all Spanish speakers, needed additional support and motivation. Many of them feel lost and unmotivated to even try to succeed in their English classes. Carol worked with her high school students to plan an interactive lesson to teach to bilingual students in the elementary school nearby. She was looking for any "evidence of attitude change toward their work, themselves or sharing."

Carol's class brainstormed ideas about what they could do with the second graders. The students decided to work with "feelings" and to make a bilingual video demonstrating different emotions and a book that the second graders could write and draw in. Carol's students improved their English as they produced, directed, and acted in the video and reviewed the scenes depicting different emotions over and over again.

When the day for the lesson arrived, Carol's students were nervous and unsure about how to interact with the second graders. In addition, the second graders were overwhelmed by the arrival of the high school students. Carol explains what happened:

> Rather than immediately pairing the very little students off with my very big students, I decided it might be best to show our video and let the little ones just get used to us being there. I think it was a good idea. I filmed as the young students watched our video and then worked with my students. They warmed up quickly to my students. The children got into drawing pictures of things that, for example, made them happy in the books my students had made. Even my "tough" guys worked well with the children and made them laugh.

Carol was excited to see the effect the visit had on her usually apathetic high school students. Many of them immediately wanted to know when they would go back. Although the students were astounded that the second graders' English was often better than theirs, Carol's students felt they could still teach them something in Spanish and something about life. In fact, the most exciting thing for Carol was that her students requested a visit to an older group at some point. When the idea of visiting an elementary school had been introduced, the high schoolers had only wanted to deal with very young children, feeling they would be intimidated or embarrassed in front of older elementary students who might speak better English. Now those same students were thinking of discussing with older students topics they considered important, such as the dangers of gangs and drugs.

When teachers like Kathy and Carol show they value the different cultures and languages their students represent, students begin to value each other and to value themselves. They begin to recognize that the different groups have knowledge and skills that can serve as important resources.

At our college each summer, at risk high school students come for an intensive 2-week reading and writing workshop called "The Learning Edge." The idea is to give students an advantage, or edge, and encourage them to consider working toward a college education. This year the teachers asked students to brainstorm on topics such as

- Wisdom: How do you gain it to make good choices?
- What is justice
- Who am I?
- He who knows what is right will do right. Do you agree?

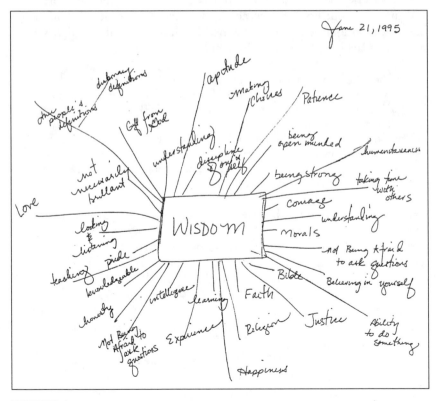

FIGURE 4.

To answer these questions, students discussed, read, and wrote. Figure 4 shows a web of ideas students created to launch their discussion of wisdom.

Many of the students this year were Hispanic and Hmong. The staff invited a Hispanic high school teacher and a Hmong elementary teacher, both with an interest in writing, to come to speak to the students. The Hispanic teacher read some of his published bilingual poetry and short stories and told the students, "You must write your stories. You have experiences that no one else has had. If you do not write them down and share them, they will be lost." The Hmong teacher told about her struggle as a refugee and the mentors who had helped her to succeed as well as her dreams to write children's books in Hmong. The students were fascinated and had many questions for the guests.

Near the end of the 2 weeks, students choose a piece of their own writing to put in a Learning Edge book to take home. The teachers were excited to see that several students wrote about their cultures and the hardships their families had endured. In addition, the students, for the first time, included poems and stories written in their first languages. The students had not only appreciated the contributions of the community resource people they had heard but they had also begun to see themselves as language and cultural resources with something important to contribute.

⊱ Goal 4: Civic Commitment Acculturation

After students experience Cortés's first three types of acculturation (mainstream empowerment, intergroup understanding, and group resource), they are ready to move on to civic commitment acculturation. Only when students feel good about themselves, see the value in their own and others' cultures and languages, and begin to draw upon all the resources around them, can they consider how to improve their communities and society as a whole.

For ESL students, it is not easy to think that they really have a voice and can make a difference in how things are run at their schools or in their communities. However, Linda provides an example with her beginning ESL students. She teaches in a large, overcrowded, inner city high school where limited funding has not only made classroom supplies difficult to get but also has postponed needed building repairs. When heavy winter rains seeped through leaky roofs into their ESL classroom, students discussed how much their school had been neglected. Following a problem-posing model (Freeman & Freeman, 1991; Freire, 1970), Linda and the students discussed what they could do about their problem. The students decided to write letters to city council

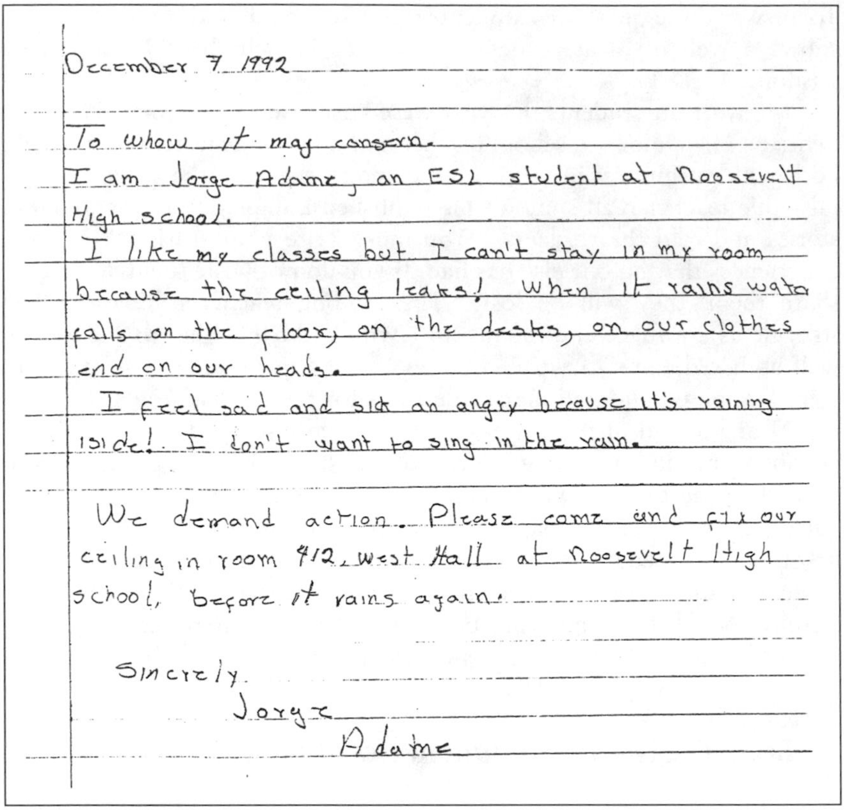

December 7 1992

To whom it may concern.
I am Jorge Adame, an ESL student at Roosevelt
High school.
I like my classes but I can't stay in my room
because the ceiling leaks! When it rains water
falls on the floor, on the desks, on our clothes
end on our heads.
I feel said and sick an angry because it's raining
inside! I don't want to sing in the rain.

We demand action. Please come and fix our
ceiling in room 412 West Hall at Roosevelt High
school, before it rains again.

Sincerely,
Jorge
Adame

FIGURE 5.

representatives, school board members, and school administrators explaining the problem and asking for the necessary repairs (see Figures 5 and 6). Jorge shows his cultural awareness when he writes, "I feel sad and sick an angry because it's raining inside! I don't want to sing in the rain." Veron-ica politely, but firmly, makes it clear that repairs are needed as soon as possible. Linda's students show Cortés's civic commitment acculturation: a willingness to act on concerns to create a more equitable society.

A final example from one of Diana's high school literature students also illustrates civic commitment acculturation. Over and over again, the examples of writing in Diana's students' books show the power that discussing and writing about topics that matter can have. Rowena Reyes, the student who wrote "A Proud People" also wrote an essay entitled, "America: A Long Way to Go" for the book *American Mosaic*. She opens her essay saying,

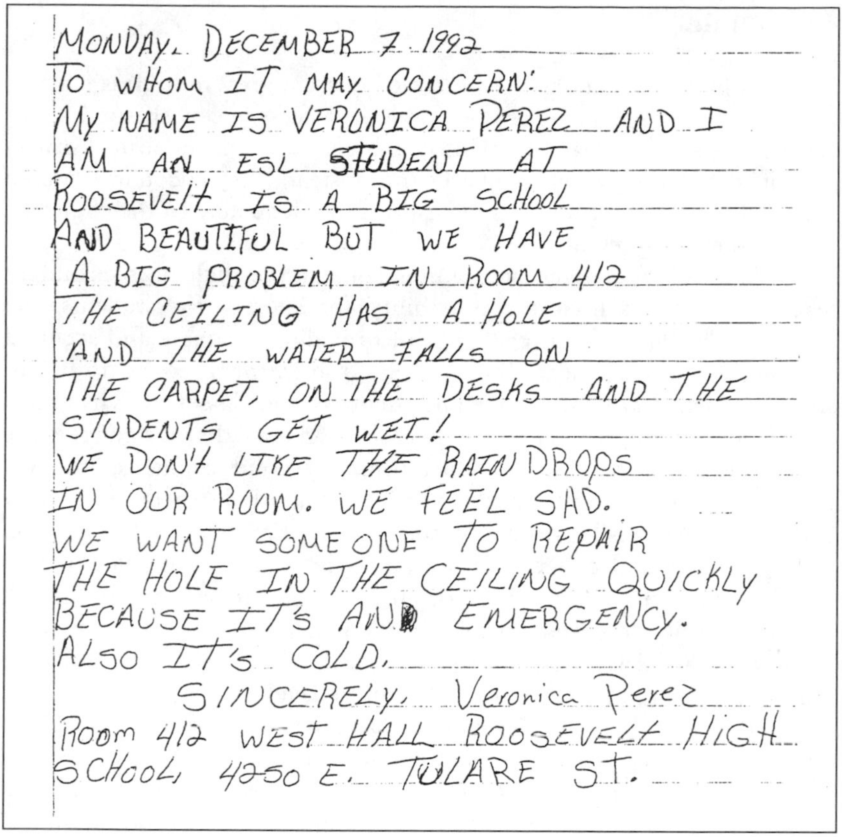

MONDAY, DECEMBER 7 1992
To WHOM IT MAY CONCERN:
My NAME IS VERONICA PEREZ AND I
AM AN ESL STUDENT AT
Roosevelt Is A BIG SCHOOL
AND BEAUTIFUL BUT WE HAVE
A BIG PROBLEM IN ROOM 412
THE CEILING HAS A HOLE
AND THE WATER FALLS ON
THE CARPET, ON THE DESKS AND THE
STUDENTS GET WET!
WE DON'T LIKE THE RAIN DROPS
IN OUR ROOM. WE FEEL SAD.
WE WANT SOMEONE TO REPAIR
THE HOLE IN THE CEILING QUICKLY
BECAUSE IT'S AND EMERGENCY.
ALSO IT'S COLD.
            SINCERELY, Veronica Perez
ROOM 412 WEST HALL ROOSEVELT HIGH
SCHOOL, 4250 E. TULARE ST.

FIGURE 6.

America, the land of spacious skies and of amber ways of grace, but that was the view of early Americans. Today, Americans are plagued by poverty, guns, crimes, discrimination, gang bangings, drugs, and other destructive problems. (p. 58)

Rowena, however, does not simply complain. She tells her readers something must be done:

In conclusion, we have seen America's problems lie in the hands of our generation. If we want our lifestyle to improve then we must start our reforms not tomorrow but today. After all, aren't we the future of America?

Rowena's essay is a clear example of civic commitment acculturation.

❧ Summary

Students like Rowena are the future of our country. In a class such as Diana's, students experience the kind of success we wish for all our secondary English learners. Unfortunately, not all English learners benefit from having teachers like Diana. Instead, they encounter limited success because schools have not responded adequately to the challenge these students represent.

We began this chapter by outlining some of the challenges secondary teachers face that limit the possibility for success for students like Rowena. They include the challenge of providing adequate and accurate assessment and placement. Too often English learners receive an inconsistent academic program. Some find themselves in classes for which they are completely unprepared and others sit in classes that do not prepare them adequately for further education. A second challenge involves developing an awareness of the needs of English learners. Secondary teachers are responsible for many students each day, and English learners who are quiet and cooperative may simply become invisible. A final challenge is to provide the kind of curriculum that will enable English learners to fully develop their linguistic and academic abilities. Students with only partial language and academic development may leave high school unprepared to succeed at the college level.

In the second part of this chapter we considered what the goals for teachers of English learners should be. Students like Rowena should not simply assimilate and fit into U.S. culture. Instead, they should add English and U.S. culture to their primary linguistic and cultural heritage. The main goal, then, for English learners is acculturation rather than assimilation. According to Cortés, we should help students develop multiple acculturation. Cortés's multiculturation model, includes four kinds of acculturation:

1. mainstream empowerment acculturation
2. intergroup understanding acculturation
3. group resource acculturation
4. civic commitment acculturation

Promoting school success for the majority of secondary English learners requires a new approach. These students pose a real challenge to the best prepared and most creative secondary teachers. Often, hard working teachers just struggle to help their English learners survive. Despite the challenges, we are advocating higher goals. As the examples we have provided show, when students and teachers work together to achieve the four aspects of multiculturation, the result can be real school success for all English learners.

✐ Suggestions for Teachers

1. Check with your school administrator or counselor responsible for testing and placement of English learners to find out how students are assessed and placed.

2. Pick out two or three English learners in your classes who are especially quiet. Arrange to interview them to find out about their family history, educational background, interests and hobbies, and hopes for the future.

3. Identify two or three English learners who appear to speak and understand English well in conversational situations but who struggle with academic reading and writing. Try to provide extra support for academic development by arranging for peer tutors, primary language tutors, or other one-on-one assistance.

4. Lead a class discussion on the difference between assimilation and acculturation and then have students write about how these concepts affect them or people they know.

5. Drawing on the examples provided in the chapter, develop a lesson or series of lessons designed to explore one aspect of multiculturation with your class.

✐ References

Alvarez, J. (1995). Who am I? In D. Cáliz (Ed.), *Voices of reflection* (p. 102). San Francisco: Balboa High School.

Chan A. (1995). Mother tongue. In D. Cáliz (Ed.), *Voices of reflection* (pp. 66–68). San Francisco: Balboa High School.

Collier, V. P. (1995). Acquiring a second language for school. *Directions in Language and Education, 1*(4).

Cortés, C. (1994). Multiculturation: An educational model for a culturally and linguistically diverse society. In K. Spangenberg-Urbschat & R. Pritchard (Eds.), *Kids come in all languages: Reading instruction for ESL students* (pp. 22–35). Newark, DE: International Reading Association.

Cummins, J. (1981). The role of primary language development in promoting educational success for language minority students. In *Schooling and language minority students: A theoretical framework* (pp. 3–49). Los Angeles: Evaluation, Dissemination and Assessment Center/California State University, Los Angeles.

Cummins, J. (1994). The acquisition of English as a second language. In K. Spangenberg-Urbschat and R. Pritchard (Eds.), *Kids come in all languages: Reading instruction for ESL students* (pp. 36–62). Newark, DE: International Reading Association.

Dooley, N. (1991). *Everyone cooks rice.* New York: Carolrhoda Books.

Dooley, N. (1993). *Todo el mundo cocina arroz.* New York: Scholastic.

Fisher-Staples, S. (1989). *Shabanu.* New York: Alfred A. Knopf.

Freeman, Y. S., & Freeman, D. E. (1991). Doing social studies: Whole language lessons to promote social action. *Social Education, 55,* 29–32, 66.

Freeman, D. E., & Freeman, Y. S. (1994). *Between worlds: Access to second language acquisition.* Portsmouth, NH: Heinemann.

Freeman, Y. S., & Freeman, D. E. (1997). *Teaching reading and writing in Spanish in the bilingual classroom.* Portsmouth, NH: Heinemann.

Freire, P. (1970). *Pedagogy of the oppressed* (Myra Ramos, Trans.). New York: Continuum.

Garland, S. (1993). *Shadow of the dragon.* New York: Harcourt Brace.

Krashen, S. (1985). *Inquiries and insights.* Haywood, CA: Alemany Press.

Liang, M. (1994). American mosaic. In D. Cáliz (Ed.), *American mosaic* (p. 1). San Francisco: Balboa High School.

Peterson, R., & Eeds, M.A. (1990). *Grand conversations.* New York: Scholastic.

Reddin, M. (1995, March 1). Adult pen pals make it their business to meet students. *The Fresno Bee,* pp. B1–B2.

Reyes, R. (1994). A proud people. In D. Cáliz (Ed.), *American mosaic* (p. 17). San Francisco: Balboa High School.

Tan, A. (1993). Mother tongue. In T. Cooley (Ed.), *The Norton sampler: Short essays for composition.* New York: W. W. Norton.

Wertsch, J. (1991). *Voices of the mind.* Cambridge, MA: Harvard University Press.

❧ Further Reading: Multicultural Literature Suggestions for Adolescents

Ada, A. F. (1993). *My name is María Isabel.* New York: Atheneum Books.

Atkin, S. B. (1993). *Voices from the fields: Children of migrant farmworkers tell their stories.* Boston: Little, Brown.

Beatty, P. (1981). *Lupita mañana.* New York: William Morrow.

Benedict, S., & Carlisle, L. (Eds.). (1992). *Beyond words: Picture books for older readers and writers.* Portsmouth, NH: Heinemann.

Bode, J. (1989). *New kids in town.* New York: Scholastic.

Brimner, L. D. (1992). *A migrant family.* Minneapolis, MN: Lerner.

Buirski, N. (1994). *Earth angels: Migrant children in America.* San Francisco: Pomegranate Artbooks.

Buss, F. L., & Cubías, D. (1993). *Journey of the sparrows*. New York: Dell.

Crew, L. (1989). *Children of the river*. New York: Dell.

Criddle, J., & Mam, T. B. (1987). *To destroy you is no loss: The odyssey of a Cambodian family*. New York: The Atlantic Monthly Press.

Dooley, N. (1991). *Everyone cooks rice*. New York: Carolrhoda Books.

Dooley, N. (1993). *Todo el mundo cocina arroz*. New York: Scholastic.

Fisher-Staples, S. (1989). *Shabanu*. New York: Alfred A. Knopf.

Freedman, R. (1980). *Immigrant kids*. New York: Scholastic.

Garland, S. (1992). *Song of the buffalo boy*. San Diego, CA: Harcourt Brace Jovanovich.

Gilson, J. (1966). *Hello, my name is scrambled eggs*. New York: Pocket Books.

Goldfarb, M. (1982). *Fighters, refugees, immigrants: A story of the Hmong*. Minneapolis, MN: Carolrhoda Books.

Hautzig, E. (1986). *The endless steppe: A girl in exile*. New York: Scholastic.

Herrera, J. F. (1994). *Calling the doves*. Emeryville, CA: Children's Book Press.

Ho, M. (1991). *The clay marble*. New York: Farrar Straus Giroux.

Hoffman, E. (1989). *Lost in translation*. New York: Penguin Books.

Howard, K. K. (1990). *Passages: An anthology of the Southeast Asian refugee experience*. Fresno, CA: Southeast Asian Student Services California State University, Fresno.

Jones, R. (1976). *The acorn people*. New York: Bantam.

Kezwer, P. (1995). *Worlds of wonder: Resources for multicultural children's literature*. Toronto: Pippin.

Kidd, D. (1989). *Onion tears*. New York: Orchard Books.

Knight, M. (1992). *Talking walls*. Gardiner, ME: Tilbury House.

Knight, M. (1993). *Who belongs here? An American story*. Gardiner, ME: Tilbury House.

Livo, N., & Cha, D. (1991). *Folk stories of the Hmong: Peoples of Laos, Thailand and Vietnam*. Englewood, CO: Libraries Unlimited.

Lowry, L. (1989). *Number the stars*. New York: Dell.

Miklowitz, G. (1985). *War between the classes*. New York: Dell.

Namioka, L. (1994). *April and the dragon lady*. Orlando, FL: Harcourt Brace.

Nhoung, H. Q. (1982). *The land I lost*. New York: Harper & Row.

O'Dell, S. (1977). *Carlota*. New York: Dell.

Rhodes, D. (1993). *The corn grows ripe*. New York: Puffin Books.

Say, A. (1996). *Grandfather's journey*. Boston: Hougton Mifflin.

Shea, P. (1995). *The whispering cloth: A refugee's story*. Honesdale, PA: Boyds Mills Press.

Silko, L. M. (1991). *Almanac of the dead*. New York: Penguin Books

Soto, G. (1990). *Baseball in April and other stories*. San Diego, CA: Harcourt Brace Jovanovich.

Sullivan, C. (Ed.). (1994). *Here is my kingdom: Hispanic American literature and art for young people*. New York: Harry B. Abrams.

Taylor, T. (1973). *The Maldonado miracle*. New York: Avon Camelot.

Thomas, J. R. (1994). *Lights on the river*. New York: Hyperion Books for Children.

Uchida, Y. (1976). *Journey to Topaz*. Fairfield, PA: Atheneum.
Uchida, Y. (1978). *Journey home*. Fairfield, PA: Atheneum.
Uchida, Y. (1983). *The best bad thing*. New York: Aladdin Books.
Yep, L. (1977). *The child of the owl*. New York: Harper Collins.
Yep, L. (1993). *Dragon's gate*. New York: Harper Collins.

Chapter ℘ 2

The Everyday Surprise: Nourishing Literacy in Classroom Environments

Carole Urzúa

One of my favorite books is *The Wednesday Surprise* (Bunting, 1989). The story never ceases to inspire me. A little girl, Anna, and her grandma read together on Wednesday nights while grandma baby-sits, plotting a surprise for the birthday of Anna's dad. When the surprise for dad becomes our surprise, and grandma, not Anna, demonstrates her new literacy ability, honed in the Wednesday night tutoring sessions, I always get tears in my eyes.

If I were teaching primary school, one of the first books I would read my class would be *The Wednesday Surprise*. And after we had cried and cheered and laughed, we would talk about how in the world this little old grandma came to learn how to read. Perhaps someone would note that she really wanted to read; she seemed to initiate the tutoring sessions. I might note that they did not have any worksheets or skill packs to finish; rather, they just sat side by side, reading books out of the book bag grandma always brought on the bus, perhaps after a trip to the library. Someone would surely note that they were really having fun because the illustrations show them laughing, and someone else would surely say, with a sense of wonder, that reading at home is often that much fun because you can talk about the books.

That is what I would do.

As I have imagined my conversation with children, I also have come to understand that part of the reason I like *The Wednesday Surprise* so much is because the environment in which literacy grows and flourishes between Anna and her grandma is consistent with knowledge about human development of literacy. Further, I am challenged to think of how to establish a classroom environment that will allow effective literacy development to take place.

29

My challenge in the next few pages, therefore, is to share some considerations that you may want to remember as you plan a classroom environment that will nourish literacy. I would like to focus on three considerations, all of which reflect knowledge of how human beings learn to language and literacy:

1. Language and literacy grow in purposeful settings.
2. Language and literacy grow as literate behaviors.
3. Language and literacy grow when they are authentic.

ᴥ Language and Literacy Grow in Purposeful Settings

One of the most important aspects about learning, and especially language learning, is that it has a purpose (Urzúa, 1980). Halliday (1973) says it best: Children learn what language is because they know what language does. Instead of controlling the situation so that students just go through the motions because they are told to, teachers who nourish literacy want their students to make their own decisions about what and how they will read and write. And, of course, there are many different reasons people, including children, read. I read to be entertained, to get information on some things I know only a little about, to add to knowledge I may know a lot about, to buttress my arguments, to see whether I agree with an author, to be moved, and to be reminded of the person who wrote, among others. I imagine some of these are the same reasons children read.

Believing that learning must be purposeful creates a whole array of possibilities for a classroom. First of all, because each person is unique, the room will have to be stuffed with texts to accommodate each reader's needs. One second-grade teacher, Debbie Manning, has thousands of books in her Fresno, California, classroom, the books as much a part of the environment as the desks. The books range from wordless picture books to easy fiction to harder fiction and nonfiction. There are 14 different magazines the class receives all lined up in library boxes, business cards and brochures on the bulletin board from people who have come to visit or talk, notes on the message board, bulletin boards that the children take turns putting up, newspapers—all of these texts available for students to read for different purposes.

Having all of those texts is important for another reason: Children who are learning English as an additional language (EAL) will need massive input in both oral and written form in order to create their hypotheses about their new language (Krashen, 1982). ESL pedagogy of the past has often been based on a belief that second language learners need less input, carefully sequenced so as to ensure the learner's success at each stage. But most of us who have learned a L2 know that the most advantageous environment was one where we were immersed in the oral and written forms. This allowed us to apply our special language processing abilities, figuring out the patterns that occurred as the language was used in real settings. It is especially important, then, to provide a wide variety of texts so that children learning EAL can become acquainted with syntax, vocabulary, and sound-symbol correspondence that may be different from what is found in their native languages (Grabe, 1991).

The literate environment of a classroom will also need to include texts of a variety of genres in the L2 because readers' background knowledge interacts with certain types of organization, and people learning another language may experience a text in the L2 in a way different from native speakers of English (Carrell, 1984). The research on the importance of genre, still in its beginning stages, can nevertheless make a big difference to our teaching of children of color, mainly because we educators will have an opportunity to look at the aspects of genre reflected in the native language/culture to make advantageous decisions for individual students. For instance, Pellegrini, Perlmutter, Galda, and Brody (1990), working with African American mothers and their children in Head Start programs, noticed that when the texts they read to their children matched the kind of texts with which they were most familiar (e.g., a local newspaper or sales flyers sent through the mail), the mothers were "more competent teachers of their children . . . than around traditional format, children's books" (p. 450). This was the case for both narrative and expository genres. (See the section on Authenticity for further discussion on the importance of understanding the home.)

❧ Implications

What are some implications of this knowledge? Perhaps you might make available a lot of materials—including books, pamphlets, brochures, junk mail, and newspapers—about subjects that are old and new to students to help expand their repertoire and that, in turn, will help them learn from the text. It is truly exciting to see how subsequent reading of a text can inform the understanding of earlier texts—and vice versa.

Perhaps some of the children in a classroom will be new learners of English. It will be helpful, then, to have a good selection of predictable books for them. How fortunate that we now have such a rich variety of repetitious texts—which is extremely important for emergent second language readers. It will be much easier for the children learning ESL to make the connections between the symbols on the page and the language connected to the symbols when they are well acquainted with the rhythm, vocabulary, and syntax of the predictable texts.

It will be important to have texts written in the L1 of the students, also, because the students already have the syntax and knowledge of the way in which their own language organizes certain kinds of texts. It will be easier to read texts in the native language, even if the students are emergent readers in the native language, because a person only learns to read once (Hudelson, 1984, 1987). And the stronger students' literacy in their L1 is, the easier it will be to incorporate reading and writing of their L2 into the processes they have already acquired in their native language literacy (Hudelson, 1987).

Many teachers are finding that a truly purposeful use of books is to share them, and encourage sharing, rather than teaching "reading." One way that may be organized is through literature studies (Peterson & Eeds, 1990).

As conceptualized by Edelsky (1988), and realized in the classroom of Karen Smith, a masterful sixth-grade teacher, there are two purposes for literature studies: (a) aesthetic responses by readers; these include understanding the world and exploring the inner worlds of feelings, impressions, intuitions, and imaginations; and (b) analytic activities by readers that include discovering the ways in which individual authors use language to disclose meaning about literary elements such as characterization, plot, setting, mood, theme, and symbolism. The teacher introduces five or six books to the class, gives a short synopsis of each book, and invites learners to choose one of the books to read silently. Then the groups meet to share their own personal meanings about the text.

The process has the flavor of a book group where people meet informally and talk about a book that they have all read. Such conversations roam far away from the text, but are always stimulated by some construction of meaning that the members make. One of the impressive aspects about literature studies is that from the conversations, in which the teacher participates as an equal responder, the group will collectively decide what question or issue would be helpful and interesting to pursue as the readers go back into the text to understand aspects of the author's craft. It appears that as students read more, they become more aware of writing styles and conventions and this, in turn, makes them better writers (Hansen, 1983). The conversations from these literature studies will certainly help children learning EAL because they will be talking about content that is really important to them as well as negotiating the meaning with other students, some of whom will also be learners of EAL. (See Urzúa, 1992, for an extended discussion of literature studies with students learning EAL; also Barto, 1992.) Children should always be helped to have access to the texts, and, if children choose texts that are difficult for them, teachers can make sure that they have a partner to read with, or maybe even a tape to listen to. By reading what interests them, readers can build on what they already know.

It was a boy named Omar who taught me the importance of individual interest. Omar was a sixth grader who, by his own admission, was trying to gain the record for the most suspensions in a school. Having failed second grade two times because "I was so dumb," and never having been in schools that saw his bilingualism as an asset, he had experienced little in school that tapped his linguistic energy. Then one day he was offered two books, *The Stranger* by Chris van Allsburg (1986) and *Dawn* by Molly Bang (1983). Both of the books centered on metaphysical enigmas; both of them captivated Omar. He read them over and over, trying to puzzle them out, because he liked them so much. They finally made sense to him so that he was able to interpret them for others. And by his own admission, "That's why I started getting into reading." Gloria Norton, the resource teacher at the school who had shared the books with him, asked him to be her assistant with the fourth-grade class when they met in small groups to discuss books. She gave him a purpose for reading, and for talking. The day I talked with him, he had just finished three books that various groups were reading; then he led a discussion on one of the books. Literacy had become real to him, and, not unimportantly, it had provided him the opportunities to gain self-esteem. I asked Omar what he would like to encourage teachers to do with children: "Read to them and make them get into books. Start them like me. Make them choose their own book, and when they keep getting bored, help them choose some books for little kids." Omar concluded, "I don't know how did I get into books, but it will be hard to get rid of books."

❧ Language and Literacy Grow as Literate Behaviors

As one thinks of what kind of environment should be present for reading and writing to grow, it seems imperative to take a step further back and ask: What are the goals? The goals should be the prime movers of the environmental responses. I used to think that "What do you want your students to be able to do in reading and writing?" was a simple question. And the simple answer was, "I want them to read and write." Then I read Heath (1984), who says our job is not to teach literacy skills, but to help students become literate, because "becoming literate is not the same thing as learning to read and write" (p. 15). So, really, the question is not, "What do I want my students to be able to do?" but rather, "What do people, including my students, already do with reading and writing that I can help them continue doing?" or "What are the literate behaviors that people engage in as they go about living, and how can I help my students do more of them in more effective ways?" Literate behaviors, then, are in part something one does as a human being and if the environment in school is "literate," then human beings will keep doing more and more of the behaviors as they/we become part of the Literacy Club (Smith, 1988).

Vuong, a sixth-grade Cambodian boy, was a picture of how literate behaviors often get confused with the demands and inferred expectations of the classroom. His ESL teacher instituted dialogue journals and in response to Vuong's query and anxiety about what to write, his teacher said to write about anything he chose, "including what you did on the weekend, if you want." Vuong's understanding of his teacher's words, framed, perhaps, by his observation that it was important to write what the "assignment" was, and that his school was interested in mechanically accurate writing, was thus translated, week after week, into a description of what his weekend entailed.

Weekend

It was Saturday I woke up and I took a shower. And after shower then I watched cartoon with my mom. My dad wasn't home. He went somewhere. When he come back he took us to my uncle house. We had dinners there. And came back to our house.

His teacher constantly interacted with him by asking expanding questions about football games, the ice storm the area had experienced, his map drawing skills, her own joy at playing soccer, and many others over a 2-month period. Each of her entries was followed by "On Saturday I . . . ." It seemed clear to the teacher and me that Vuong was engaging in literacy skills experiences. It was possible, for instance, to look at his writing and note that he had mostly well-formed sentences, appropriate spelling, indentation, and other conventional forms. But was he really writing?

Fortunately for Vuong, his teacher continued to encourage him to see writing as sharing his ideas with an interested audience. Finally, 2 months later, the teacher asked him about his violin playing, and Vuong wrote, "My favorite piece is Lightly Row I been playing for 2 years." Recognizing his responsibility for maintaining a written conversation, not simply practicing his writing skills, Vuong finally engages in a true literate behavior, the same one that he might engage in as he writes letters to friends or answers questions on an application—activities people outside of school really do (see Urzúa, 1987).

Part of what developing literate behaviors means, then, is to nurture that which is done naturally by humans when engaged in purposeful learning. The other part of developing literate behaviors is to "learn to talk reading and writing" (Heath, 1985, p. 15). That talk must come from the collaborative experiences, written and oral, that teachers and students have together, such as being able to speak and write about a variety of experiences, or to explain and sequence implicit knowledge and rules of planning.

One such event, where students are learning to talk reading and writing, is a cross-aged tutoring program begun in Stockton, California, by sixth-grade teacher Barbara Cook and first-grade teacher Mary Stirton. (See Cook & Urzúa, 1993, for a manual on how to establish this project.)

In this project, half of the older students, self-named as the *Rapid Readers* (RR), go to the classroom of the younger students, referred to as the *Little Readers* (LR), and vice versa. Each RR pairs with an LR after being trained in ways to talk about books, to write lesson plans, to figure out what to do when helping someone who is learning to write, and other things they need to know to be successful. The older students are in total control of these sessions, planning and managing activities. Each session, lasting from 30 to 40 minutes, is followed by the RR returning to the classroom and reflecting on the process by writing field notes. The class members then discuss issues of teaching they have encountered, and each RR plans for the next session.

Although it may seem as if the cognitive and linguistic demands for the RRs are high, one of the underlying principles of this program is that all children will participate. Now, several years later, the elementary school where the program takes place enrolls 75% language minority children, mostly refugees from Southeast Asia. On occasion, there have been RRs who were just beginning their English odyssey themselves. But the program founders believe that to become literate, the children must learn to talk reading and writing as they themselves teach behaviors they are often just learning. Often the language they use will be the L1 of their LRs as they engage in literacy events by reading predictable books (many of which are practiced by RRs as they themselves gain access to text) or as they write together. RRs often use the L1 to translate passages they believe will be troublesome to the LRs, to ask questions and talk about the text, to maintain discipline, to create new stories, and much more. As they negotiate content in meaningful ways, the L1 will be strengthened, which will, in turn, help strengthen the learning of a L2.

The literate behaviors in which both sets of children are engaged are made conscious for the RRs through experiences consistent with the goals established by Cook (see Cook & Urzúa, 1993):

1. Gain confidence in yourself.

2. Be aware of the knowledge you have so you can share it with others.

3. Be a good observer.

4. Be able to record what you've seen.

5. Be aware of your Little Reader's needs, and be able to adapt to those needs.

6. Plan and carry out your plans.

7. Keep learning about the literacy process so you will become a better reader and writer. (p. 3)

These goals are visible in the ways in which the RRs interact with their LRs. But they are highly visible in the writing and discussing that the RRs do after their teaching experiences.

Here, for example, are some field note entries that demonstrate how conscious of the literacy process the RRs are becoming. One RR reflects on his recent experience and then makes plans for what he will do differently next time:

10/5/89. My little reader was very jumpy today. He was running around in the class. he read just a little but mostly he was playing around. He would get a book and he would not want to read it and he would go get a different one. Before we had left he had[n't] read one whole book. Next week I will try to act out the book. He will probably like that. I will also have him act out parts . . . . when he is interested in the book he will really sit down and read.

Here is an example of an RR who is learning about the writing process and applying it to her LR.

1/8/90. She know how to spell some words but if she can't spell a word, I always encourage her to spell her best.

Sensitivity to learning needs is evident in this entry:

10/24/91. "My LR read a book with me. the book was called <u>The Seed.</u> This was a short book. That's why I chose this book to read to my LR."

Viewed over a school year, the growing confidence of the RRs is evident in the changes that take place in the writing they do. Xe, for instance, a Hmong girl who enjoyed school and was outgoing personally and academically, demonstrates her growing knowledge of literacy by using her writing. She is tentative at first, and constantly uses the disclaimer *I think* . . . in front of her statements of belief.

> 11/2/91. I think she will make it easy for me to teach her all the skill for to read and write.

In November, she makes an entry that appears to be written to her LR:

> Yes, some words are clues. You have to look at the picture and then sound the first letter out and you could read the word. You would find clues very easy. You can find clues in the piture or in the sentence.

Her confidence is evident here as well as her theory of reading, (one that was not necessarily espoused by the teacher who might urge less attention to graphophonics). But by the spring, all traces of her disclaimers have disappeared, and her entries sound like a manual for literacy:

> She know how to spell some words but if she can't spell a word, I always encourage her to spell her best.

> I told her to read two books I chose and I also asked her to tell me about the books on Tuesday. I did that because I want to know if she know how to read.

38 Implications

Besides trusting that children learning an additional language are capable of engaging in processes such as dialogue journals and cross-age tutoring, what are some concrete ways in which your own teaching environment can reflect work on literate behaviors? Perhaps the most obvious—and potentially powerful—is to demonstrate your own literate behaviors:

- Share your own reading with children, pointing out why you chose a certain book, what parts were more difficult and why, what parts you loved.

- Share your writing as well, composing in front of children, reflecting out loud about your processing.

- Bring examples of your own writing.

- Participate in writing conferences with students, revising your pieces and publishing ones you like.

- Encourage students to talk about how they are processing their reading and writing; establish a community sharing time when readers and writers talk about the strategies and expertise areas they are using when they read and write.

Helping children see what people truly do in the Literacy Club is the best motivation for becoming a member.

ða Language and Literacy Grow When They Are Authentic

What have been your literacy events of the past few days? Here's a list of mine:

- I left a note for the painter fixing our bathroom.

- I sent a fax to my editor about changes in an article I was publishing.

- I wrote a thank-you card to my sister-in-law acknowledging a book she sent me.

- I read the political sections of a news magazine to share ideas with my like-minded friends.

- I began a new novel by Gail Godwin.

- I read through several Christmas catalogues.

- I read an article on Chronic Fatigue Syndrome.

In all of these literacy experiences, I have made decisions based on my needs as well as those of the people with whom I was interacting. My events have been purposeful and self-motivated, and I have utilized many of my literate behaviors (e.g., I expected my texts to make sense; I wrote and read differently depending on my audience and purpose; I scanned some things and read slowly for others). I was engaged in authentic literacy.

And so the third criterion for a rich literacy environment: authenticity. Our goal as educators is to create literacy events that are as comfortable within the four walls of the classroom as they are outside. If the experiences and decisions readers and writers are making inside the classroom are significantly different from those made outside, then the events may not advance literacy.

I find this criterion the most difficult to understand and implement. It requires me to see the classroom as an extension of community life, but I have spent my student and much of my professional years being socialized and viewing the classroom as a unique culture, carefully nurtured and protected by authorities, both people and materials, apart from the community. I find it even more difficult because, even though many educators have moved to literature-based instruction in the past decade, I struggle, and I know they do, too, to perceive new roles for themselves and their students. For example, numerous manuals exist for the "teaching" of pieces of children's literature (some many times longer than the rest of the book itself) such that teachers make most of the decisions about how, what, when, and why students will read and write. Even when teachers move to theme cycles, we try to make all the connections long before students begin the experiences, and end up planning what and why students will write (e.g., an autobiography because the theme is "All about Me,") and read (e.g., a not-so-literary book about Helen Keller because the theme is about courage).

All of these decisions must lie in the hands of readers and writers if they are to be engaged in authentic literacy.

And so as we come to the most inclusive criterion for a successful environment for language and literacy to flourish, we also come to the one that will require the most changes in our theory and practice. We will have to be willing not just to "let" students read and write, but to nurture the very life of literacy. A life needs many things in order to grow, but I would like to share two: space and time.

❧ Space and Time

Literacy needs space; in fact, it needs a variety of spaces. We all have developed emotional attachments to certain places where literacy has grown: My favorite place to read is in bed. Cambodian monks read sitting on mats in a *wat* (temple). A French hotel clerk who checked me in sat at the registration desk with a stack of magazines.

Classrooms, too, can offer a variety of spaces for students. In our practice of literacy we may include lofts and cubicles, pillows and bean bags, rocking chairs, couches, and mats for readers to lie on. Space outside classrooms should be used as well—chairs moved outside, blankets spread under trees. Some spaces will reflect a reader's need to privacy, and other spaces will encourage side-by-side reading.

In addition to space, much time is needed—long, blocks of time, free from interruptions. There is nothing as pleasurable for me as an afternoon in which I turn off all of the bells and whistles in my house, get a new Ann Tyler novel and a big glass of iced tea, and let myself be taken to new worlds. Long chunks of time have always helped me get the most from my literacy experiences outside of school.

Inside of school? How frustrated we all have been at the fracturing that schools do with scheduling, pulling apart connections learners can make simply by not providing long enough time slots. But where can we find the time and space needed to make literacy experiences authentic in school? How will we be able to provide the massive input needed for both oral and written acquisition, perhaps more even for L2 literacy than for L1, given the structures we have now in school?

Life- and literacy-giving teachers have those difficulties, too, so one thing they do is expand literacy input time to include home time. Not home*work* time, but literacy activities and practices that are "integrated into the fabric of daily life . . . becom[ing] a rich resource that can inform rather than impede learning" (Auerbach, 1989, p. 166). Every culture and every household have these activities and practices and, therefore, the time children are immersed in literacy input is greatly increased.

When students, especially those learning an additional language, receive a message that there is a "literacy time" in school for an hour, from 9:15–10:15, listed on the schedule as *reading*, they begin to distrust the literate behaviors they may be developing. The process is analogous to 5- and 6-year-olds who have acquired the complexities of their native tongue coming to school to face lifeless texts of language that do not reflect what they already know. Because the school promotes these texts as reading, many children grow to distrust the authentic language knowledge they already possess and they begin to treat the text as the true knowledge.

So it is with learning or acquiring an additional language. Homes have provided access to text, even text in the mother tongue, but school sometimes does not recognize the burgeoning life of literate behaviors. Research of the past decade has substantiated a number of beliefs that demonstrate that, for many families, literacy is as integrated into their lives as eating and sleeping are. It is so important that we learn to recognize this integration because we often are confused by claims to the contrary. Auerbach (1989) lists five myths about literacy in homes of low-income and minority students, and then dispels those myths.

1. One long-standing myth is that in low-income homes, limited resources and nonreading adults create "literacy impover-ished" homes. The facts, however, show that families use a range of literacy practices, value literacy development, and

often systematically reward literate behaviors (Chall & Snow, 1982; Taylor & Dorsey-Gaines, 1988). Strickland (1991) shares her belief that families often engage in nonnarrative literacy events (as when an uncle takes his niece and nephew to get a dog license) and concludes that "even in families where storybook reading may not be a regular event, learning together abounds. As with obtaining a dog license, much of that learning is linked to literacy" (p. 8).

2. A second myth concerns the directions of literacy instruction, as historically practiced, namely from adult to child in a "natural" transmission. The facts, however, indicate that children, particularly children of immigrant parents, assume a complex series of roles, including ones where children read and translate for their parents (Tizard, Schofield & Hewison, 1982). Additionally, when instructed to read in English to their non-English-speaking parents, children actually scored very high on English reading achievement tests, due undoubtedly to the social dynamics of literacy events and the rich discussion about the texts in their L1 that the families must have conducted (Tizard, Schofield & Hewison, 1982).

3. A third myth concerns the misplaced recognition that certain homes prepare successful children for schools by direct instruction on narrow school tasks. The facts demonstrate, however, that a wider range of literacy contexts and home experiences more generally correlate with "successful" readers, and that parents, even immigrant parents, who embed language and literacy into their daily life actually help their children to a wider range of literacy achievements (Taylor, 1981, 1983).

4. A fourth myth concerns the belief that literacy instruction that takes place at school is the more natural or accepted, and that homes need only reinforce school practice for achievement to occur. The causes of reading success or failure are then attributed to what happens in the home. The facts, however, show that the match between literate behaviors at school as well as home work together to provide success in literacy (Heath, 1983; Urzúa, 1986).

5. A final myth concerns a school's perception that belief systems of immigrant groups need to be "overcome" and changed to more "mainstream" views for their children to be successful in school. The facts are that attitudes of parents toward schools and toward their children's own literacy matter far less than

the lack of social, political, and economic support for parents to carry out healthy lives that will affect social contexts (Taylor & Dorsey-Gaines, 1988). A related issue is discussed by Caplan, Choy, and Whitmore (1992). After interviewing more than 200 refugee families who had been in the United States fewer than 3 years, they concluded that the emotional ties between parents and children, the cultural validation and wisdom shared in mother tongue stories, and the value placed on reading and learning were much more predictive of academic success than the English production of the parents. In fact, those parents who recognized the importance of maintaining their own cultural heritage instead of adapting to U.S. culture exclusively had children who did better in school.

The gentle reader of these myths may honestly be asking, "But what do these beliefs have to do with an authentic environment nurtured by time and space?" For me, the sociocontextual and cultural factors of literacy reflect attitudes that in turn affect the environment and, therefore, recognizing what these factors are, and celebrating the literacy that is already present in each household of our children will help us to make more out of school experiences accessible to our students. Auerbach is persuasively reminding us that authentic literacy experiences do happen, even in homes that we may not understand as well as we do our own, in activities we would all recognize as developmentally appropriate: Space is often found for homework activities (e.g., when Hmong refugee families set up a table for working, but eat by sitting on the floor), and time is often set aside for making sure all assignments are done. As we become more familiar with the socialization patterns in families of our students, we will, perhaps, be more confident that we can extend literacy to the home with the knowledge that the activities will be but extensions of what they already do.

❦ Conclusion

Remember one of my favorite books, *The Wednesday Surprise*? I love the book, partly because of the way in which literacy grows and flourishes between Anna and her grandma. As I have shared thoughts in this article about a rich classroom environment, I hope you have had an opportunity to reflect on how that growth between the two was consistent with the three areas I have explored: language and literacy growing in purposeful settings, as literate behaviors, and in authentic experiences.

I first examined what may be the most obvious: that language and literacy grow in purposeful settings. Grandma learned to read because she wanted to surprise her son; she had a strong purpose. Perhaps she also wanted to show the two younger children that it is always possible to learn to read and, still again, she may have finally given in to the yearning to become literate. The purpose, however, really drove the activity. It drove Anna's activity as well—how excited she was to know that she had a significant hand in Grandma's new ability.

Secondly, I examined the ideas that language and literacy grow as literate behaviors, not as literacy skills. Anna did not bring home workbook activities for Grandma to engage in; even at 7 and "smart as paint," Anna knew access to lots of books was going to be the key to Grandma's success. Grandma undoubtedly made many trips to the library or, perhaps, even to a bookstore, as she seems to have brought all of her books on Saturdays. Those activities seemed natural to both Anna and Grandma. My only regret is that I was not present when the two began cooking up this idea, and Anna began planning for how her teaching would unfold.

Finally, I examined the idea that language and literacy, indeed, all of learning, grow when they are authentic. Anna and Grandma's culture appears to be one in which stories are read while people sit on couches. The stories are most often fiction, meant to entertain, and occasionally to inform. In Anna's culture, it is acceptable for a younger person to teach an older person and performing one's skill is embedded in the family contexts. Anna's choice of pedagogical tools was consistent with what her own cultural literacy beliefs were.

All of these aspects of a rich environment are present in the teaching context, and, thus, Grandma is successful. May there be a special Anna in all of our lives, in the lives of our students and their families.

℘ Suggestions for Teachers

1. Train yourself to recognize a continuum of literacy events that can take place anywhere, anytime.

    *   Bring in third-class mail daily and make it a part of classroom libraries.

    *   Collect and exchange coupons in a place in the classroom. Parents who have been invited, often through home visits, to contribute their cultural and personal expertise, are thrilled by such an exchange. (Strickland, 1991, reports on how Lois Scott does this in her Detroit classroom.) Children can be encouraged to observe and document

literacy events in their communities, homes, and schools.
(See Heath, 1984, for a description of one such project.)

2. Support and become knowledgeable about family literacy
   projects that see themselves as more than transmission of
   school culture and literacy skills to poorly functioning adults.
   These literacy projects use literacy to address social and
   political problems, child-rearing concerns, and interaction with
   school systems in a genuine dialogue as well as celebrating
   and developing the home language and culture. In the
   Harvard Family Literacy project, for example (Auerbach,
   1989), teachers attempted to:

   - model whole language activities that parents might do
     with children (e.g., telling stories or making books)

   - validate culture-specific literacy forms (e.g., reading,
     writing, and telling folk tales and proverbs)

   - explore parenting issues (e.g., exchanging letters with U.S.
     parents in an adult basic education program or writing
     letters of advice to pregnant teenagers in a high school
     program)

   - address community, workplace, and health care issues
     (e.g., responding to pictures of different educational
     settings in terms of their own educational experiences and
     expectations for children's education)

   - practice advocacy in dealing with schools (e.g., writing
     letters about concerns to children's teachers)

   - explore political issues (e.g., writing language-experience
     stories about the elections in Haiti)

   Another noteworthy project is Project FIEL (Family Initiative
   for English Literacy), whose goals include enhancing biliteracy
   and parental self-confidence to empower participants to
   connect literacy activities to their own social and cultural
   situations (Quintero, 1991).

3. Encourage parents to send to school texts, or suggestions for
   texts, that they want to read and that they want their children
   to learn how to read. Encourage parents to engage in written
   dialogue with you and their children, in a roving journal. Dan
   Doorn and teachers in Las Cruces, New Mexico, working
   with Mexican American children, encouraged the use of
   home-school journals that the children wrote at home, often
   with the input of parents, and brought to the class to share
   (Doorn, 1995).

4. Make a special effort to elicit information from parents for ongoing assessment. The *Primary Language Record* (1989), for instance, recommends parent input through interviews about such items as their child's favorite books at home, differential use of both languages, and writing interests. All of this information can help teachers make harmonious decisions about literacy events at school. Often through being asked the questions, parents will be made even more aware of their own literacy events, and a more open communication system may result.

5. Visit churches and synagogues for donations of books. Ask community people to share with parents and students how literacy functions for them in their daily life. Whenever possible, demonstrate your own literate behaviors and ask parents to demonstrate theirs. One teacher brings her child with her on home visits and brings a bag of the child's books that someone eventually hauls out for everyone to read, with the parents then showing how they might conduct similar events.

6. Find places in the community where children and literacy can flourish. For example, in an innovative project in Las Cruces, New Mexico, Dan Doorn and his colleagues (personal communication) have put narratives and poetry of Mexican American and Native American children on place mats that are copied, laminated, and distributed by parents to local restaurants. One project I coordinated made place mats for a church; the place mats are used at potlucks and other events where members would otherwise have had no contact with the children.

7. Demonstrate how literacy informs all your life, particularly the stories of your life, by writing family and personal histories and sharing the process and product in your classrooms. Often such demonstrations lead to children sharing their own stories. Many such stories are being written and published by teachers who share time and space with children learning additional languages. Anthologies have been published by the Portland, Oregon, ESL/Bilingual program (*The hills of home: A collection of folk stories by the Mien community*); by the Chinle, Arizona, Navajo reservation of Chinle Junior High; by bilingual high school students at Stagg High School in Stockton, California; and by elementary students at William T. Machan school in Phoenix, Arizona.

ⓘ References

Auerbach, E. B. (1989). Toward a social-contextual approach to family literacy. *Harvard Educational Review, 59*, 165–181.

Bang, M. (1983). *Dawn*. New York: William Morrow.

Barto, D. (1992). *Literature studies with high school students*. Poster session presented at the 26th annual convention of TESOL, Vancouver, Canada.

Bunting, E. (1989). *The Wednesday surprise*. New York: Clarion Books.

Caplan, N., Choy, M., & Whitmore, J. (1992). Indochinese refugee families and academic achievement. *Scientific American*, pp. 36–42.

Carrell, P. (1984). The effects of rhetorical organization on ESL readers. *TESOL Quarterly, 18*, 441–470.

Chall, J., & Snow, C. (1982). *Families and literacy: The contributions of out of school experiences to children's acquisition of literacy*. A final report to the National Institute of Education.

Cook, B., & Urzúa, C. (1993). *Come to the literacy club: Cross-age tutoring and paired reading*. Washington, DC: National Clearinghouse for Bilingual Education.

Doorn, D. (1995). Family collaboration in children's literacy: When journals travel home. In G. Weinstein-Shr & E. Quintero (Eds.), *Immigrant learners and their families*. Washington, DC: Center for Applied Linguistics.

Edelsky, C. (1988). Living in the authors' world: Analyzing the authors' craft. *California Reader, 21*, 14–17.

Grabe, W. (1991). Current developments in second language reading research. *TESOL Quarterly, 25, 375–406*.

Halliday, M. A. K. (1973). *Explorations in the function of language*. London: Edward Arnold.

Hansen, J. (1983). *When writers read*. Portsmouth, NH: Heinemann.

Heath, S. B. (1983). *Ways with words*. Cambridge: Cambridge University Press.

Heath, S. B. (1984). Literacy or literate skills? Considerations for ESL/EFL learners. In P. Larson, E. Judd, & D. Messerschmitt (Eds.), *On TESOL '84: A brave new world for TESOL* (pp. 15–28). Washington, DC: TESOL.

Hudelson, S. (1984). Kan yu ret and rayt en ingles: Children become literate in English as a second language. *TESOL Quarterly, 18*, 221–238.

Hudelson, S. (1987). The role of native language literacy in the education of language minority children. *Language Arts, 64*, 827–841.

Krashen, S. (1982). *Principles and practice in second language acquisition*. New York: Pergamon Press.

Pelligrini, A., Perlmutter, J., Galda, L., & Brody, G. (1990). Joint reading between black Head Start children and their mothers. *Child Development, 61*, 443–453.

Peterson, R., & Eeds, M. (1990). *Grand conversations: Literature studies in action*. Ontario, Canada: Scholastic/TAB.

Primary language record. (1989). Portsmouth, NH: Heinemann.

Quintero, E. (1991). *Project FIEL*. Washington, DC: Office of Bilingual Education and Minority Language Affairs.

Smith, F. (1988). *Joining the literacy club*. Portsmouth, NH: Heinemann.

Strickland, D. (1991). Making connections: Home and school. *Teacher networking: The Whole Language Newsletter, 10* (4), 1, 8–9.

Taylor, D. (1981). The family and the development of reading skills and values. *The Journal of Research in Reading, 4,* 92–103.

Taylor, D. (1983). *Family literacy.* Portsmouth, NH: Heinemann.

Taylor, D., & Dorsey-Gaines, C. (1988). *Growing up literate.* Portsmouth, NH: Heinemann.

Tizard, J., Schofield, W., & Hewison, J. (1982). Symposium: Reading collaboration between teachers and parents in assisting children's reading. *British Journal of Educational Psychology, 52,* 1–15.

Urzúa, C. (1980). *Speaking with a purpose.* Lincolnwood, IL: National Textbook Co.

Urzúa, C. (1986). *A children's story.* In P. Rigg & S. Enright (Eds.), *Children and ESL: Integrated perspectives* (pp. 93–112). Washington, DC: TESOL.

Urzúa, C. (1987). "You stopped too soon": Second language children composing and revising. *TESOL Quarterly, 21,* 279–304.

Urzúa, C. (1992). Faith in learners through literature studies. *Language Arts, 69,* 492–501.

van Allsburg, C. (1986). *The stranger.* Boston: Houghton Mifflin.

✌ Further Reading

Crago, M. B. (1992) Communicative interaction and second language acquisition: An Inuit example. *TESOL Quarterly, 26,* 487–505.

Ochs, E. (1988) *Culture and language development: Language acquisition and languages socialization in a Samoan village.* Cambridge: Cambridge University Press.

Heath, S. B. (1989). The learner as culture member. In M. L. Rice & R. L. Schiefelbusch (Eds.), *The teachability of language* (pp. 333–350). Toronto: Paul H. Brookes.

Phillips, S. U. (1983). *The invisible culture.* New York: Longman.

Scollon, R., & Scollon, S. (1981). *Narrative, literacy and face in interethnic communication.* Norwood, NJ: Ablex.

Vogt, L., Jordan, C., & Tharp, R. (1987). Explaining school failure, producing school success: Two cases. *Anthropology and Education Quarterly, 8,* 276–286.

Chapter ℘ 3

Cross-Age Tutoring and ESOL Students

Katharine Davies Samway and Carlyn Syvanen

℘ A Buddy Reading Program in Action

There is a hum of excitement in the upper grade classroom, even though it is neither Halloween nor the day when a famous singer is to visit the school. In fact, this excitement, revealed in the glances of anticipation some students direct at the door and impatient queries, "*When* are they coming?" is not unusual in this classroom, particularly on Tuesday mornings right after recess when the class buddies up with a primary class from the other side of the grey concrete patio that separates two wings of classrooms. The teacher is finishing up a short lesson on how to read nonfiction picture books to young children, and as she glances at her watch, one of the students calls out, "Here they come!" In minutes, half of the children in the upper grade class have exchanged places with half of the primary class, and pairs of children are immersed in books.

Many of the children are acquiring English as a nonnative language. In some cases, children are speaking together in a language other than English, for example, Spanish or Laotian. In other cases, the common language is English, and the children's speech patterns reflect those of nonnative English speakers. Some children are reading books written in English, while others are reading bilingual books or books written entirely in a language other than English. In some pairs, the older child does most, if not all, of the reading, whereas in other pairs the younger child does the lion's share, or the two children divide the reading between them, taking turns to read. Some children spend time at a listening table where they hear books on tape, following along in their own copies. Some children read big book versions of their favorite stories.

49

After about 20 minutes of reading and talking about the books that each child has brought, some of the buddy reading pairs are writing and drawing in their literature logs, a place for them to record their reactions to the books they have read together. In some pairs, the younger children draw and then dictate their messages to their older scribes. In other pairs, both children are writing together, and, periodically, they glance over at each other's work and comment on what they see. After about 30 minutes, their teachers, who have been walking around their respective rooms, listening in, making observations, and offering help, announce that the children have a couple more minutes before the buddy reading session is over. Children glance up, look over at the clock, groan, urge each other to hurry up, and eventually say their good-byes.

Upon returning to their respective classrooms, the two groups of children engage in a debriefing, a chance to reflect upon what happened and what they learned from this weekly cross-age tutoring event. The primary children congregate on the large rug that is located near the big book easel, pocket chart and blackboard and launch into a discussion:

Teacher:	So, how did it go today? Did you have a good time?
Students:	Yes. Yeah. Uh huh. (Some nod) (Speaking together)
S1:	I read one book.
Teacher:	Uh huh. What did you read?
S1:	Brown Bear.
S2:	I read that. The big book. That one.
Teacher:	Oh, the one we made. Okay. That's great that you read one of our books. Did Alejandro like it?
S2:	He laugh. He like the picture.
(Pause)	
Teacher:	Who else would like to tell us about their buddy reading?
S3:	Mines was good. I read. She read. Like this. (Demonstrates with another student how she and her buddy both held the book.)
S4:	It was okay. I didn't like my book.
Teacher:	Why was that? Why didn't you like it? Are you talking about the book you selected? You chose?
S4:	Yeah. My book. It was too long.
Teacher:	Uh huh. It was too long for you. So what made you decide on that book?
S4:	(Shrugs her shoulders)
Teacher:	Was it a book you knew already?
S4:	(Shakes her head)
Teacher:	Okay, maybe that's the reason why it wasn't a successful book for you. Boys and girls, it's a good idea to choose books that you know. It's important to take books that you really want to read.

S5:	(Interrupting) I liked my books. These are great books. They're funny, real funny. Look at this. (Holds up a small book version of Mrs. Wishy Washy) Look at the pig's big butt! (Laughter as the children point to the picture of the pig, who is trying to sit in a washtub).
Teacher:	Yeah, it is funny, isn't it? (More laughter) And how about you, Margarita, did you have a good buddy reading time?
S6:	(Nods her head and holds up three books, two written in Spanish, *Voy al Dentista* and *Mis Coshaceres*, and a Spanish/English bilingual book, *Uncle Nacho's Hat*).
Teacher:	All right. So, you took some books that you've really enjoyed reading with Mrs. Alvarez? (Referring to the Spanish speaking instructional aide)
S6:	(Nods her head again). Sí. (*Yes*)
Teacher:	Great. (To the entire class) That's a great strategy. To take books that you know and love. That way, you can have a more successful experience as it's much easier to read a book if you're really familiar with it. Do you remember last week when I read that book to you without reading it first and I had such a hard time and kept stumbling over the words?
Children:	Yeah.
Teacher:	But once I'd read it, I could read it much better the second time? It's the same for you, right?
Children:	Yeah. Uh huh.
S7:	I knowed this book and it was easy. Pon tell me I'm a good reader. She did this when I read it. (Imitates how Pon gave him a hug)
Teacher:	So she was proud of you when you read it and gave you a hug?
S7:	Yeah.

The conversation continues in this way for a few more minutes, with children sharing their successes, problems, and concerns. The teacher makes a note on her pad to check up on a couple of pairs the following week, to make sure that their difficulties are not deep-seated. She makes a mental note to check with the upper grade teacher, too. She also makes a note about the need to teach the children once again about strategies to use when selecting books. Although not all the children are having problems choosing appropriate books, she will probably address the entire class so as to be able to draw upon children's successful experiences. At the end of the oral debriefing, the children go to their tables where they spend the remaining 10–15 minutes before lunch drawing and writing about their buddy reading experiences of that day.

In the upper grade classroom, the older children begin their debriefing by writing in their journals. A television crew had been visiting classrooms filming footage for a program on schools and they filmed the buddy reading session. Brenda, a fourth grader from Mexico who came to the United States when she was in second grade, comments on these visitors and then remarks on what she and her buddy did and how her partner behaved:

> today one buddy's ther was this man cmaren peple in buddy's room and he topt me and aftur We wor finchede we came back to our cellas so did he and hes storeing to teck peckare to us. but in The buddy's class we med some anumos and it was fun My buddy did lisen tome

> [Today on buddies there was this man camera people in buddy's room and he took me and after we were finished we came back to our class so did he and he's starting to take pictures to us. But in the buddy's class we made some animals and it was fun. My buddy did listen to me]

Angelina, a sixth grader who also came from Mexico, writes about her buddy's behavior and learning processes. She comments that her buddy pays more attention when she, Angelina, reads on a topic that interests the younger child:

> I notice that my partner was pay more atetion to the book about fish. I asked what she like about it and she said that she liked it because she was still interested in fish and she was going to make a play or some thing like that. I was glad that she was pay atetion beause I get mad when they don't pay atention.

Fifth-grader Lance, a native speaker of Chinese, lists a range of teaching strategies that he used when working with his buddy:

> Today I put the book right in the middle and he start to read to me. We took turn reading too. Like he read one book I read one book.

Choulaphone, a native speaker of Laotian, writes about difficulties her younger buddies experience when confronted by unfamiliar words:

> The thing I learn from buddy reading that I knew that Amy and Mel remember the words and when they go back to the words then they point to the old one and then they say say it and they kept on doing that and when they come to a word they don't know then they ask me and I say alittle bit of the word and they just say it and they keep on reading.

Azucena, a fourth grader who has been in the United States for about a year and is literate in Spanish, has always written her weekly entries in Spanish—until today, when she elects to write in English. She comments on how she handled her younger partners who were copying what she was writing:

> today I went to the class of are buddys and I read a book baut were I play and I tell my buddys you net to rait baut waht to you like to playd traw a picture baut what to you like to playd and I was toing my worck and my buddys was copin me and I said you net to do your worck you not pustu capenme and April said Bu I want to copeyou OK bu you net to raide baut watt you like to playde.

> [Today I went to the class of our buddies and I read a book about where I play and I tell my buddies you need to write about what do you like to play draw a picture about what do you like to play and I was doing my work and my buddies was copying me and I said you need to do your work you not supposed to copy me and April said But I want to copy you. OK. But you need to write about what you like to play.]

After about 10 minutes, the class begins to debrief orally. They talk about the degree to which buddy reading was successful. They raise concerns and offer suggestions. Sometimes students glance at their journals, as if to remind themselves of what it was that they wanted to share. As the bell for lunch sounds, they put their journals away and in some cases continue their conversations about their younger buddies: whether or not they paid attention, how much they liked the books, and what to do with acutely shy children who hardly say anything.

🎐 The Context for This Scenario

The buddy reading scenario that we have just shared is a composite of many cross-age reading sessions of which we have been a part. In this chapter, we draw upon our experiences working with elementary-age students in two different contexts: a pull-out fourth-/fifth-grade ESOL class in Portland, Oregon and a regular fifth-/sixth-grade class in Oakland, California that was made up of children speaking a variety of native languages, including English. We will focus on the effects of a cross-age literacy experience on the older students (the tutors).

🎐 Effects of a Buddy Reading Program on Students

We have found that cross-age tutoring is very effective with elementary-age students who are acquiring English as a nonnative language, regardless of how fluent they are in English or how experienced they are as readers and writers. This is true for students who are at the beginning stages of English, but literate in their native language, fifth graders such as Diana and José, both recently arrived from Mexico. These two students had well-developed literacy skills in Spanish, but did not know much English. They received half an hour of ESOL and half an hour of Spanish pull-out classes each day, but for the rest of the day, they sat in their fifth-grade classroom trying to understand what was happening around them. As part of their ESOL class, they had the opportunity two afternoons a week to work with Spanish-speaking first graders from a bilingual classroom, children who were developing literacy skills in Spanish.

Diana seemed very shy and hesitant in her other classes, tending to hang back and never answering questions unless she was very sure that she was right. However, when she walked into the cross-age tutoring classroom, she would stride in confidently, gather up her materials, and volunteer for various tasks. She was quick to meet her partner and immediately got down to the business of reading books or writing stories. She was a confident, resourceful learner and teacher in the cross-age tutoring sessions.

The same was true for José, who was a reluctant reader in English, but a very fluent reader in Spanish. He would read with tremendous expression and when he was reading books in Spanish, other tutors and their younger partners would often stop what they were doing to listen to him reading. His expertise in this context was obvious, yet it was an expertise that had not been revealed previously in his English-medium classroom.

This aspect of older ESOL students having such successful language and literacy experiences in the buddy reading context is quite striking as we noticed it over and over again. We believe that the successful cross-age experience for tutors is attributable to the following three influences:

1. opportunities to be experts, something they rarely experience in English-medium classrooms as newcomers to English

2. occasions to express and develop interpersonal and teaching skills

3. experiences with English print that are authentic and comprehensible

Being Experts

Because of their lack of fluency in English, ESOL students rarely experience pride in what they do during most of the school day. Instead, they are constantly reminded of what they are not able to do. We have seen how paralyzing lack of success can be on students' academic growth and self-esteem. It is often difficult for teachers to orchestrate learning events in which ESOL students can be as successful as their more fluent English-speaking peers. We have found that buddy reading can provide the kind of risk-free environment that allows ESOL students to be experts, albeit for a relatively short time each week. Their expertise is frequently grounded in the fact that they are often more fluent in English and more fluent readers and writers than their younger buddies, in the native language and in English. The fact that the older students are in an expert (vs. novice) role during buddy reading seems to enhance their confidence and sense of accomplishment.

Developing Interpersonal and Teaching Skills

Students' expertise extends beyond being more fluent in English or being more skilled as readers and writers, however. We have noticed that many of the students show remarkably good skills as teachers. They are often patient, attentive listeners; they frequently address inappropriate behavior calmly, directly and without put-downs; they respond favorably to the opportunity to help someone else succeed; and they take great pride in the accomplishments of their younger partners and in their own accomplishments as teachers.

The tutors recognize that they have an affect on their younger buddies, and this is often revealed in their assessments. A sixth-grader, Viliphone, commented in her written reflections, "I think that the thing that I like best about buddy reading program is that we get to open up each child when we talk about the book each week." Choulaphone wrote about her buddy's reaction to her being late for buddy reading: "When I went to Ms. Pippitt class I saw her (Mano) all lonly and when I went in she was so happy that she saw me." Both Viliphone and Choulaphone recognize and appear to value the degree to which they are having an affect.

As a consequence of the buddy reading experience, students have an opportunity to develop their interpersonal skills, which is reflected in fifth-grader Roberto's comment on the relationship he had established with his buddy: "Karl my buddy is reading good. I treet him like if he was my son and [he] treets me like a dad." When we have surveyed students about the buddy reading program, many students comment that they believe that they are more effective teachers than adult teachers. Ronald, also a fifth grader, wrote the following:

> They even talk more when they are meeting with us. They even understand more abut the book that they are reading. Like I said, they feel more comfortable reading with kids near their age. When they read with grown up they don't feel so comfortable.

Tutors frequently express the belief that younger learners share their thoughts more freely with them because they are closer in age.

Having Authentic and Comprehensible Experiences With Print

Even when students are literate in their native language, reading and writing in English can be a challenge, particularly as they move into the upper grades where texts are longer, less dependent on pictures, and more complex. For some ESOL students who have been in U.S. schools for 3 or more years without benefit of native language instruction, reading and writing in English can be even more stressful. Nadya, a fourth grader from Russia who started her schooling in the United States in first grade, is one of these students, and her classroom teacher was very concerned because she could not read at all. In her pull-out ESOL class, she began to work with a first grader who also spoke Russian. Although they read books written in English in this cross-age program, the children often used Russian when talking about the texts. In the preparation period, when students chose the books they were going to use and practiced reading them to a partner, Nadya was very self-conscious about not being able to read and so chose to read with her ESOL teacher. She chose predictable texts and slowly built up a repertoire of books that she became comfortable reading. In the process of preparing for the cross-age experience, she developed her own reading fluency. Whereas Nadya had once been a rather self-conscious and reluctant tutor and reader, she eventually became one of the most enthusiastic tutors and a more fluent reader.

In many cases, tutors do not have access to buddies who speak a common language other than English. In these cases, English becomes the medium for communication. We have noticed how, when this happens, buddy reading provides a very effective way for students to listen to and use English in a relatively stress-free context. In order to prepare for each buddy reading session, fourth- and fifth-graders Paco, José Luis, Deborah, Mara, and Alonzo, all native speakers of Spanish and newcomers to English, would choose the books they wanted to take with them to their meetings with their buddies. At first, they would listen to a peer tutor reading a relatively simple predictable book once, twice, three times, or more. Then they would practice reading the book to each other. Then they would practice reading these books to more fluent English speakers. They would also take home tape recorders, picture books, and audiotapes of the stories to practice listening and reading in English. We have found that because students are rehearsing for an authentic session with another person, they are very committed to engaging in all this practice prior to reading to their buddies. During buddy reading, students focus on the content of the books, rather than the grammatical forms or vocabulary, as is still often the case in ESOL classes. The greater informality of the buddy reading setting seems to free the tutors to process language and use English to whatever extent they are comfortable.

🍃 Tutors' Reactions to Buddy Reading

We have noticed that tutors often progress through stages in their reactions to buddy reading. In the early stages, their reactions to the buddy reading experience are often euphoric, as this journal entry from sixth-grader Barbara, reveals:

> Well Buddy Reading whent great. he could read very good and he really whanted to listen to the story he drawed very well and write good he wrote like this I LIK ET and I was really proud of him Well the book he mostly talked about more was the Three Billy Goats Gruff. He really likes book that has adventure and action he is great.

Later on, however, we notice how students' comments are more typically lamentations or complaints about the behavior of their tutees (e.g., "When I ask him if he want to read a book he say no," or "today my buddy reader was bad because when I read to him he play around"). These types of comments remind us of the experiences of new teachers who often become preoccupied with behavior management issues. This preoccupation with behavior and discipline became a focus of several of Barbara's "middle stage" entries, as the following illustrates:

> Well buddy reading whent a littel wild because my buddy was a littel wild. He didnt whant to read he just read one book and the rest of them he said they where all boring. I tried to tell him which book did he whant to read but he just kept on talking to Choulaphone and wouldn't let her read with her buddy we really didn't have a discussion going on at all well thats all

After students have had many opportunities to discuss their difficulties, and after their teacher has taught them about developmental learning stages and appropriate instructional strategies, students' comments frequently reveal a greater sense of reflectiveness. Instead of simply blaming their buddies for everything that goes wrong, they begin to comment on the impact of their instructional decisions on student learning. In the following journal entry from Barbara, she comments on how pointing to the text and providing continuous encouragement seemed to help her partner and made for a satisfying session:

> Well Buddy Reading today whent great he was really reading the book everey time I pointed to the think (*thing*) that it said in the book he will read it he felt very proud of himself and he wrote in his journal he wrote: I LK WN E WS OD TREE and I kept on encouragin him so he won't feel bad because he was kind of shy. Well my buddy payed attention 100%. he really was showing interest in the book. Me and my buddy din't have no problems at all.

℘ Implementing and Maintaining a Successful Buddy Reading Program

Successful cross-age programs do not happen miraculously overnight. In fact, we know that they require a great deal of effort. We frequently talk with teachers who have had experience implementing cross-age programs. In some cases, they have been very successful. In many cases, however, they quickly abandon their cross-age programs. Sometimes, it is because their teaching partner is not equally committed to the concept. In other cases, the children do not really understand the purpose of the program or their respective roles, and lose enthusiasm. In still other cases, the teacher jumps into the program without adequately preparing the students, and the tutoring sessions degenerate into directionless, often chaotic free time. We have learned that establishing and maintaining a successful cross-age program requires a great deal of thought, preparation, and commitment, and when these features are in place, the chances for success are much improved. Our experiences tell us that the following five features are critical for the successful launching and maintenance of a cross-age program.

Initial and Ongoing Preparation of Both Groups of Children

We have found that both groups of children need to be prepared for working together. In the case of the younger children (the tutees), this preparation may include teaching them about attentive listening strategies, how to select books, and how and where to store books in the classroom (e.g., book bins or shelves for wordless picture books, big books, books about animals, science magazines, poetry, bilingual books, and books in languages other than English). In the case of the older children (the tutors), preparation may include becoming knowledgeable about a wide variety of picture books and magazines (fiction and nonfiction), reading strategies used by emerging readers, stages of developmental spelling, read-aloud strategies, understanding and attending to inattentiveness, and strategies for working with children who are acquiring English (e.g., using lots of gestures, facial expressions, acting out, and objects to convey meaning; questioning strategies that take into account varied levels of fluency and understanding in English) and when to use these strategies (e.g., in the case of children who are newcomers to the language, asking questions that only need a nod or a shake of the head in response). We have worked with older students who are very inexperienced readers. When they are told that they will be helping younger children learn how to read, they become very anxious, and it is only when they are introduced to books written for emergent readers (e.g., short texts, predictable elements) that they relax. Through demonstrations, we show them how to read these books and how to help younger children read them. As students often practice reading the books several times before introducing them to their buddies, they have opportunities to become more fluent readers through reading books that they would usually not choose to read in case they are stigmatized for reading "baby books."

Time for Students to Reflect After Each Cross-Age Meeting

Both groups of children need to have frequent opportunities to reflect, in writing and orally, so that they may learn from their experiences and from each other. These times for reflection should follow as soon after the buddy reading session as possible. We have found these sessions to be very helpful to the students, but also to us as teachers. Through listening very carefully to their comments and the issues they raise, we are able to make instructional decisions. For example, when sixth-grader Vanessa repeatedly mentioned that she was having difficulties with her buddy Danielle (e.g., "My partner doesn't like to read and when I ask her what happened in this part she says, 'I don't know.' She's not paying attention."), it was clear that an adult needed to carefully observe Vanessa's interactions with Danielle the following week. It became quickly apparent that a Danielle that we had not known before existed. Teachers had previously viewed her as a resistant learner and inexperienced reader. The observations revealed that Danielle was, in fact, a very energetic and enthusiastic reader, but her tutor, Vanessa, was inadvertently putting her down through sighs and yawns and repeated corrections of Vanessa's oral reading miscues. We use these kinds of data when deciding on the content of whole-class minilessons and conferences with individual students.

Teachers Electing to Work With One Another

The teachers must want to work together and should both be enthusiastic about the project. Teamings should not be mandated. The teachers should keep in close contact with each other, planning, sharing observations and insights, and discussing concerns. The most successful programs that we are familiar with share these characteristics. Sometimes, an impressed administrator may mandate that all teachers need to embark on a cross-age program. This can lead to disastrous results as a successful program can be quite time-consuming, even while it is very satisfying for both the students and teachers.

Collections of Appropriate Books in Both Classrooms

Both classrooms should have a fairly extensive collection of books and magazines appropriate for the younger children. In this way, reading materials are immediately available during buddy reading sessions. In addition, the children can prepare themselves for future sessions throughout the week. Books should be in English, in languages other than English, and there should also be bilingual books, whenever possible. It would be a mistake to limit the selection to only fiction, however, as many children enjoy reading nonfiction books, magazines and newspapers. Also, books and magazines written by children need to be shelved alongside commercially published texts. A wide range of genres is also desirable—we have found that primary children particularly enjoy predictable texts (both big book and regular size versions), wordless books, poetry, rhymes, information books, and books written by their tutors.

Pairings of Students

Cross-age partnerships should remain constant, at least for several months, so that the children can get to know each other and be willing to take risks. If a pair is not working out, the teachers need to discuss the problem with the students and, if there is no workable solution, offer an alternative pairing. Many of the children can be paired randomly, but there are likely to be situations where it's important to think very carefully about who is matched with whom.

Tutors often feel that they can do a better job if they work with children from the same language group. Students explain that it is easier to help someone understand when they can use their native language. When trying to match by language background, it sometimes works out that siblings or cousins work together—in our experience, this has not led to any serious problems.

It is not always possible to match students by language background, however. When this happens, we have found it helpful to take the following factors into consideration.

1. Reading fluency: We generally pair younger readers who are not reading independently with tutors who are strong readers.

2. Personality: This is a rather subjective matter, but it can make or break a partnership. We have found that a quiet tutor often works best with a buddy who has a similar personality.

3. Attendance: Because it is difficult for students who are placed with buddies who miss a lot of school, we usually pair students who are frequently absent in triads.

4. Student's requests: When children make special requests, as often happens in multiage classrooms where students are with the same teacher for more than one year, we try to honor their requests in order to help cement the bond that was formed in the previous year.

5. Behavior: It is not unusual for some of the younger students to engage in verbal put-downs, hitting, biting or teasing, or to have difficulty staying on task. When this is apparent, we try to match the students with tutors who are mature and able to work particularly effectively with younger children.

We should point out that we do not think that it is wise to apply any of these factors in a rigid way.

❧ Suggestions for Teachers

If you are interested in establishing a successful cross-age tutoring program, you may want to consider the following recommendations.

1. Find a teacher with whom you can buddy. The benefits of tutoring seem to be greater if there is at least a 2-year age gap

between the tutors and the tutees. It helps a lot if you share a similar philosophy about learning and teaching with the other teacher.

2. Carefully select a time for the cross-age tutoring session that is not affected by minimum days, assemblies, and holidays. Students need to know that they will meet together each week at a regular, predictable time. This means that if you teach in a multitrack, year-round school, you and your partner will have to be on the same track.

3. Allow for 20- to 30-minute cross-age tutoring sessions. We have found that sessions that go on longer than 30 minutes tend to lose their focus. Fewer than 20 minutes do not really give students enough time to get into their work together.

4. Weekly sessions seem to work best. Students have often asked for more frequent sessions, but, when held once a week, cross-age tutoring remains a special, much-anticipated event.

5. Allocate 10–30 minutes before each cross-age session for preparation. The amount of time allocated for preparation will depend on your goals. For example, if all you need to do is to conduct a focused minilesson, then 10 minutes is usually sufficient. However, if you want students to also select books and practice reading with each other prior to meeting their buddies, then 30 minutes is reasonable.

6. Schedule 20–30 minutes after the cross-age session for students to write in their journals and orally debrief. The journal writing is important so that each student has an opportunity to reflect upon the experience. Try to read as many of the entries as possible as it helps one stay in touch with all students, not just those who are willing to speak up in the large-group debriefing session. The oral debriefing session is important as students do a lot of problem solving at this time.

7. During the cross-age tutoring session, walk around, observing, listening in, keeping anecdotal records, and noting topics for future minilessons.

8. Minilessons may focus on a range of topics, and should be grounded in the needs of the students. The following list reflects some of the more common issues that we have addressed in minilessons:

   • how to praise younger learners/brainstorming words of praise

- how to help others learn
- how to choose books
- developmental stages of spelling/what to expect in younger learners' writing
- developmental stages of reading/how to help emergent readers
- how to get to know one's buddy
- the role of questions/questions that lead to rich discussions
- how to read aloud effectively
- how to handle inattentive students
- favorite authors and illustrators

We have found that brainstorming and role playing are two strategies that work particularly well in addressing these topics.

9. Get ready to be delighted as you observe how the older students become highly motivated and responsible teachers and the younger students become more attentive learners.

໖ Further Reading

Cook, B., & Urzúa, C. (1993). *The literacy club: A cross-age tutoring/paired reading project.* Washington, DC: National Clearinghouse for Bilingual Education.

Heath, S. B., & Mangiola, L. (1991). *Children of promise: Literate activity in linguistically and culturally diverse classrooms.* Washington, DC: National Education Association.

Juel, C. (1991). Cross-age tutoring between student athletes and at-risk children. *The Reading Teacher, 45,* 178–186.

Labbo, L. D., & Teale, W. H. (1990). Cross-age reading: A strategy for helping poor readers. *The Reading Teacher, 43,* 362–369.

Leland, C., & Fitzpatrick, R. (1994). Cross-age interaction builds enthusiasm for reading and writing. *The Reading Teacher, 47,* 292–301.

Morrice, C., & Simmons, M. (1991). Beyond reading buddies: A whole language cross-age program. *The Reading Teacher, 44,* 572–577.

Samway, K. D., Whang, G., & Pippitt, M. (1995). *Buddy reading: Cross-age tutoring in a multicultural school.* Portsmouth, NH: Heinemann.

Chapter 4

Achieving Literacy Through Multiple Meaning Systems

Kathryn Z. Weed and Monica A. Ford

The long, accordion-folded butcher paper was stretched along the wall. Each panel contained a picture drawn by a child in the class. The book that had inspired the children's work was *Goodnight Moon* (Brown, 1947). Under each picture were the words *good night* and the name of the object the child had drawn. When I (Kathy) entered the room about 20 minutes before class officially started, Ana, an English language learner, and Dave, a native English speaker, were moving along the panels, pointers in hand, reading the captions. They stopped to discuss the picture for those captions they did not know and would sometimes discuss the various authors whose names were on their respective drawings. A few minutes later, Tommy and Olga, two other English language learners, read through the "book" with their pointers. "Goodnight, Mom," "Goodnight, Dad," they read together.

In kindergarten classrooms where language is honored, and stories, songs, chants, and poems along with play corners, puzzles, blocks, and trucks fill the day, children find themselves immersed in rich everyday and academic language. In such classrooms, various symbol systems are employed to lead children to literacy. A common practice is one as described above in which a story provides the impetus for a drawing, the drawing inspiration for a new story or sentence completion (as in the case above); the drawings later become a class book. Interaction, discussion, and problem solving are all components that lead to the finished product and, as evidenced by Ana and Dave's behavior, are components that continue afterward.

Inspired by such work and their own success, students may also generate their own drawings and ask to have their words dictated. In

February, 6 months after she had started school, Teeda, a Cambodian child, brought me a series of drawings on small yellow slips of paper. Over the morning, as I listened and transcribed, she produced more and more elaborate stories. Given the opportunity, Teeda was able to work out her ideas about hearts, people, safety, warmth (see Figure 1).

A.

This the small heart in the mommy. She don't want out her mommy. She still want las her mommy. She still scared and she still warm. And that's all.
Feb. 5, 1990   Mrs. Weed

B.

This you in the heart
Feb 5, 1990   Mrs. Weed

C.   2/6/90

You watch the star and my cuspin must take me home back and the bird said bye-bye to the rainbow and me was say bye-bye to the rainbow and

the bird cry.
Mrs. Weed

FIGURE 1.

But these examples are of kindergarten children. What happens to those who come to school in the intermediate grades? If Teeda, after 6 months in a kindergarten where she sang, read, wrote, drew, and interacted with other kindergartners (both in English and in Cambodian), was able to produce simple stories (in line with those of her native-English-speaking counterparts), what can be expected of a child who enters school in later elementary grades? What opportunities are available for them to participate in language-rich environments? And how do teachers provide such environments when faced with the mandate to cover the curriculum?

℞ Our Educational Beliefs and Classroom Practices

In this chapter, we examine classroom practices in Monica's multigrade (2, 3, 4), multilingual (Spanish, English, Samoan, Tongan, Armenian, and Indonesian) elementary classroom. One of the procedures that Monica uses immerses children in literature and language through the multiple meaning systems of listening and discussing, sketching, and writing. Importantly, this procedure is not an isolated, do-it-on-Friday type of activity. It is embedded in the educational environment that Monica provides. It is a practice that we advocate and that Monica finds effective because it is consistent with our beliefs about language learning, literacy, and teaching.

We believe, as Peregoy and Boyle (1997) state, that for learners to become fully proficient in a language, they must develop a repertoire of oral and written language skills from which they can choose in order to participate in the full range of social and academic situations. We believe, along with Wells (1990), that students must develop the mode of "'literate thinking' that is the most vital for full participation in a literate society. For unless individuals develop strategies, as readers, for constructing and critically evaluating their own interpretations of texts and, as writers, for using the texts they create to develop and clarify their understanding of the topics about which they write, they remain dependent on others to do their thinking for them" (p. 14).

We believe that learners are guided to language (and academic) proficiency through use of their L1; that the modes of expression in their home language are a rich and valuable resource; and that enhancement, not just acceptance, of the home language leads to fully integrated individuals and academic success. Inclusion of the learners' home languages in the learning environment sends the message that the learners—not just the learners' languages and cultures but the learners themselves—are respected and valued (Altwerger & Ivener, 1994; Legarreta-Marcaida, 1981; Wong Fillmore, 1990).

To achieve the goals of language acquisition/development and literacy, we have examined various classroom practices and developed some of our own. We have considered what adults report when asked about the role language plays for them in learning ("read and follow directions," "listen and mimic," "explain," "oral language and written skills," "verbal interaction" [personal communications, 1995]) and concur with those classroom discourse researchers who advocate opportunities for children to explore ideas through talk. "Talking is the principal means by which children show us that they can think and solve problems" (Dudley-Marling & Searle, 1991, p. 60). We find commonalities between Barnes' (1992) notion of *exploratory talk* and *final draft* and the writing process approach to written proficiency. Exploratory talk is a groping toward meaning:

> It is usually marked by frequent hesitations, rephrasings, false starts and changes of directions . . . . it is very important whenever we want the learner to take an active part in learning, and to bring what he learns into interaction with that view of the world on which his actions are based. That is, such exploratory talk is one means by which the assimilation and accommodation of new knowledge to the old is carried out. (p. 28)

We have also examined Cummins' (1981) framework of two continuua that are used to describe the language demands placed on second language learners. These continuua consider language tasks to range within "context-embedded" to "context-reduced" situations and from "cognitively-undemanding" to "cognitively-demanding ones" (see Figure 2).

Chamot and O'Malley (1987) include specific language and content activities in the Cummins' framework. We have used activities involving art, music, drama, and movement—disciplines that are often considered appropriate for beginning-level language learners. These alternative meaning systems, however, are powerful systems that help students conceptualize and lead to deeper understandings of cognitive tasks. Thus, if these contextualized systems can be used along with the students' L1, the students' English language and literacy skills are enhanced (see Figure 3).

Literate thinking is not just linked to letters and words, but "all modes of symbolic representation constitute a text, including oral accounts" (Mercado, 1991, p. 173). As Cohen and Gainer (1995) state, "Symbolic representations of the environment though [sic] pictures and

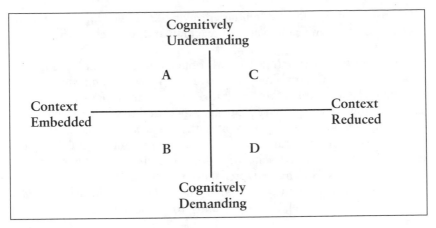

FIGURE 2. Cummins, 1981, p. 12.

sculpture are as natural to human beings as the development of speech. In fact, children's understanding and use of visual symbols frequently precedes speech and always precedes written language" (p. xv). We have found that other teachers, working with both language majority and language minority students have found art to be a means for children to express themselves and to lead them to print (Franklin, 1989; Gallas, 1994; Igoa, 1995). And we believe with Murray (Foreword to Ernst, 1994) "[c]hildren know what writers know: we write what we see. The

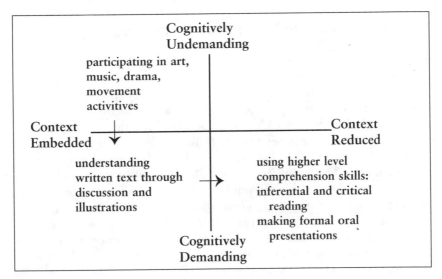

FIGURE 3. Chamot & O'Malley, 1987, p. 238.

relationship of seeing and telling, drawing and writing, is intimate, essential, and a significant aspect of teaching and researching the writing act" (p. vii).

In order to provide students with opportunities for multiple uses of language and literate thinking, to move them toward English language proficiency and literacy, yet capitalize on the meaning systems they already know—their primary language, their abilities to represent ideas pictorially—Monica uses quality literature as a springboard. She provides a variety of opportunities for learners to respond to that literature (California State Department of Education, 1994) through various meaning systems. She has adapted Harste, Short, and Burke's (1988) "Sketch to Stretch" strategy to give all students, regardless of their English proficiency level, the opportunity to participate and learn in her classroom.

In the next section, Monica describes her daily work in language and literacy focusing on the "Sketch to Stretch" strategy. Through the children's activities discussed and presented here, the reader will see the many ways in which ideas are generated, developed, and recorded; the various opportunities for oral interaction that help learners develop appropriate discourse strategies; the shared reading and writing activities that lead to literate thinking. The learners, we have found, are becoming proficient. They are developing their literacy practices. And they are doing this through their L1 and their pictures, two meaning systems they come to school with, in order to generate, clarify, and expand ideas.

❧ Multiple Meaning Systems in Action

As part of our immigration unit, the children and I read *How Many Days to America?* (Bunting, 1988). Because so many of the children had immigrated to our southern California community, they had a lot to share about their own experiences. Our discussion focused on the types of transportation that they had used and how long their journeys took.

Prior to reading our next book, *If You Sailed on the Mayflower in 1620* (McGovern, 1969), we looked at a detailed poster of a drawing of the Mayflower. This familiarized the children with the different parts of the ship and the story we would be drawing, talking, writing, and. reading about. Our discussion centered around the conditions of living on a ship in such confined spaces and for such a long period of time.

I then started the story. After reading a segment, I stopped and asked the children to draw what they thought was most important about what they had heard. They knew they were to quickly sketch their main ideas and that they could go back later to add details (similar to the writing process in which one does a rough draft capturing one's thoughts and later goes back to edit). We continued reading and drawing for several days.

At the end of each daily reading and sketching session, the children got together in groups. One by one they showed the drawing they had selected to share. The other group members gave their interpretations of the sketches, what they thought the artist intended, before the artist talked. The artists had the final say, explaining their intent. Because students were of varying proficiency in English, their sketches would capture what they understood. Concepts not quite clearly grasped could be discussed in the group and often resolved—or, better yet, would provide a context for all group members to clarify their understanding. For example, José understood the line "They played games at the first Thanksgiving." His drawing (see Figure 4) shows games taken from his own experience. He did not necessarily know which games the Pilgrims had played, but through his drawing he was able to demonstrate his understanding that Pilgrims had played games. In his group, the children discussed whether the games José had drawn were played during that time. José was a contributing member of the group; he was able to

FIGURE 4.

interact and demonstrate his understanding, and his understanding helped the other children clarify their concepts about early America.

During this small-group time, I rotated among the different groups and prompted where necessary, "What more can you tell me about your picture?" "Why did you decide to include this detail?" "Why do you think your friend had that interpretation of your drawing?" (in situations where one group member had given an original interpretation, often quite different from that of the other students). "What could you do differently to make your ideas clearer?"

Although the text and my questions were in English, the students' discussion ranged across languages. Often, a long exchange occurred in Indonesian or Spanish or Tongan. In the following example, Esteban showed his picture and the caption: *Da ledr* (the leader).

Peer group:	Who was he? (English)
Esteban:	The leader of the Pilgrims. (Spanish)
Peer group:	What did he do? (English)
Esteban:	He's the one who gave them the ideas and wanted the Indians to join them. (Spanish; forcibly)
Teacher:	What are you going to write about your picture now? (English)
Esteban:	I'm going to say that he was the leader and he got the Indians to join them for the first Thanksgiving. (English)

The students were sorting out ideas, clarifying their interpretations, and then choosing their words for their written work.

In listening to their talk, even in another language, I found it to be hesitant, imprecise, full of pauses, *ums*, and *ers*. As Barnes (1992) states, this exploratory talk occurs in situations in which the talkers feel comfortable in their explorations. I was not concerned about these primary language explorations for, I knew from my experience, the students were gaining rich conceptual knowledge through their talk and that notions understood through the English medium were being massaged and expanded in the primary language.

After their discussions, the artists wrote a sentence or two about the drawing, pulling from their own and their group members' ideas. For example, José, mentioned above, wrote "The Indians and Pilgrims plaed games at the frist Thanksgiving" (spelling by José). These first writings were most often in the student's primary language.

By the end of the week, the children had a series of drawings in a folder. They reviewed their drawings and took out those that included their writing. They got into groups again and collectively sequenced their pictures. They were creating their own book based on the story of the Mayflower.

More discussion went on during this group work. Although the published work would be in English, pairs and trios of students continued to discuss in their primary languages and the braver, sometimes the more proficient, would present ideas in English to the entire small group. I often saw three- and four-way conversations—discussion in the L1, tentative idea-presenting in English, some exploring among members in English, with questions and discussion going back and forth in various primary languages.

During the selection of pictures to sequence in their story, if two pictures were close to the same topic, the children talked about which one captured the idea better or which one had clearer written work. This discussion became a form of self-evaluation because students had to make decisions about what was to be included. Such discussion and evaluation leads directly toward Well's (1990) notion of *literate thinking*. From their initial story map, the children elaborated on their writing, adding details and clarifying thoughts. The editing evolved in a natural manner as students prepared their story for publication. They also refined their artwork, adding details, checking the poster, going back to the book for ideas. For example, Sandra's drawing (see Figure 5)

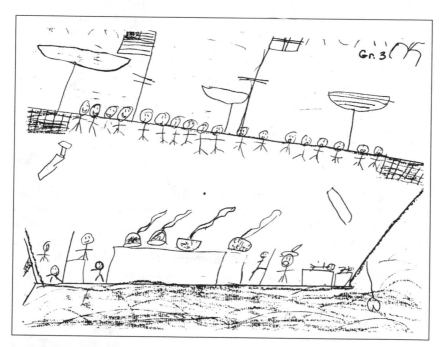

FIGURE 5.

included several different events in the single scene: lots of people on the ship, people dying on the ship, the ship anchored (showing they had arrived perhaps). Sandra was also one of the more proficient students, and we found that those students with more proficiency understood more and were able to add more specific details to their sketches. Thus, their drawings were a clue to their developing understanding as was their talk and their writing.

Throughout this sequence of activities, the children generated ideas through different systems. Writing would prompt new ideas for pictures, and pictures generated new ideas for writing. Discussion clarified, suggested, and supported. Sometimes students would even completely change a picture based on a new understanding. Other times they changed the writing. I noticed that often the shyer student was important in generating ideas for a group. The student would present an idea to another same-L1 group member. That student would then present the idea(s) to the group, and the group was off and running. If the shyer student had not felt comfortable thinking and presenting ideas in her L1, not only would she be the poorer, but so would the group.

Esteban is one of these shy students. He was classified at the lowest level of English proficiency. His drawing (see Figure 6) captures a single idea, the concept of a leader. In explaining in Spanish his drawing about the leader, the other children expanded on the leaders in the story. Esteban was thus able to expand his own understanding of the story at a point that was meaningful to him and helped all of them with a fuller understanding of leader.

During the editing sessions, I introduced small strategy lessons depending on the group's needs. These lessons focused on issues, questions, dilemmas that had come up in the natural course of discussion and writing. In this manner, we could address specific skills in the context of the students' writing.

When the final products were ready, a representative from each group read their book aloud and showed the illustrations. These students were not always the most proficient in English, but those whom the group decided would best represent them. This was a chance for some of the outgoing, natural actors to shine. For example, Carmen aspires to be an actress. Although she had only average English proficiency, she represented her group's story well through her animated reading and dramatic showing of the illustrations. The books were then placed in the classroom library for all to read. These student-produced books were so popular that they often wore out.

FIGURE 6.

TABLE 1: CONTINUUM FROM BRAINSTORMING THROUGH PRESENTATION IN THREE MEANING SYSTEMS

Meaning system	Brainstorming	Drafting	Presentation
visual (art)	sketching	adding artistic elements	illustration
oral	exploratory talk L1 and L2	clarifying talk L1 and L2	oral presentation L2
written	first writings L1 and L2	revising/editing L2	published work L2

❧ Learning About Language and Literacy

By examining the experiences of the children, we find parallel processes for the different meaning systems used in this strategy. Each of the three systems (art, talk, writing) follow a continuum. We have divided the continuum into three parts—brainstorming, drafting, and presentation (see Table 1).

Throughout this classroom experience, the children used several means to arrive at the expression of their ideas through writing. In the brainstorming, idea-gathering stage, they heard a story. They formed ideas and sketched them (sketching). They discussed their ideas in whichever mode was comfortable for them, that is, primary language, primary language mixed with English, or English (exploratory talk). The new or more developed ideas were written down (first writings). During the drafting stage, students revisited their sketches and writings. They selected sketches to use and refined them (adding artistic elements). They continued to discuss, elaborate, question, argue (clarifying talk). Their written work was affected by the clarification process of the other two systems and reflected further thought (revising/editing). These processes continued until the presentation stage in which the final product, an illustrated book, was read aloud (illustration, oral presentation, published work).

❧ Summary

Teachers are buffeted by so many demands, and to face a classroom in which some of the children do not even speak the teacher's language can be completely daunting. However, a teacher provides an environment of acceptance and exploration when she believes that children

- must be actively involved in their own learning
- learn by explaining, informing, justifying, comparing, describing, proving, debating, persuading, and evaluating
- have multiple means at their disposal to engage in the above experiences, including a rich primary language, and observation and drawing skills

Children are free to express ideas—through art, talk, writing—and to learn.

In Monica's classroom, through use of multiple meaning systems, children can more easily capture abstract ideas. They are freed from any initial concern about the mechanics of writing—an area often overemphasized early in instruction and one that can block the creative, generative flow of ideas. Writing and reading remain parts of a seamless whole in which ideas have primacy and the development of ideas follow a natural continuum from exploration to formal presentation. Children move through exploratory stages in several meaning systems to arrive at a finished product that includes those same systems. In exploring concepts through multiple meaning systems, students see areas of strength in each other. They are artists, authors, and presenters. They begin to honor each other's contributions and seek out those who have talents they lack as they support each other's literacy development. A true community of learners is created.

❧ Suggestions for Teachers

The following is a suggested sequence of experiences that guide language learners from brainstorming through drafting to presentation using multiple meaning systems (adapted from "Sketch to Stretch" in Harste, Short, & Burke, 1988).

Brainstorming

1. Reading and listening

Read selection and stop at appropriate points in text. Reading can be done by teacher, buddy, cross-age tutor, or group member. Factors to consider include student familiarity with topic, conceptual load in the text, language difficulty, and student proficiency.

2. Thinking and drawing (sketching)

Students think about what they have heard/read and then sketch "what the selection meant to me or what I understood from the reading." Students need to become aware that there are many ways of representing the meaning of an experience and that they are free to experiment with their interpretation. Students should not be rushed but given ample time to draw and refer to the selection.

Repeat Steps 1 and 2 to end of selection.

Depending on length of selection, students will produce one or more sketches. At the end of the reading period, students can select the sketch that they want to share in a small group.

3. Discussing sketches (exploratory talk)

Each artist shows her sketch to others in the group. The group members study the sketch and say what they think the artist is attempting to say. Once everyone has been given the opportunity to provide an interpretation, the artist provides his intended meaning. Further discussion may follow. This discussion occurs in whatever language the children can best convey their meaning.

4. Putting ideas on paper (first writings)

After discussion, the artist writes a sentence or two about the sketch incorporating her own and group members' ideas. This first writing will often be in the student's primary language.

Drafting

5. Selecting

From the collected sketches, each student selects the one(s) to take to final draft.

6. Clarifying talk, artistic elements, and revising/editing

In a small group, the students sequence their sketches. They discuss the resulting "story map," elaborate on their sketches by adding details, and revise their writing. Students should have plenty of time during this phase because they are enhancing their ideas by moving back and forth among these meaning systems (visual, oral, and written) (See Table 1).

Presentation

7. Compiling sketches and writing

Final sketches and written work can be compiled into a published book. Books produced by using this process can be authored by individuals, pairs of students, small groups, or whole class.

8. Making final products public (illustration, published work, oral presentation)

Children may be given choices as to how they want to share their work. A few ideas include reading aloud to their own or another class, inviting parents and reading to them, presenting the book to the school library, dedicating books to another classroom.

✌ References

Altwerger, B., & Ivener, B. (1994). Self-esteem: Access to literacy in multicultural and multilingual classrooms. In K. Spangenberg-Urbschat & R. Pritchard (Eds.), *Kids come in all languages: Reading instruction for ESL students* (pp. 65–81). Newark, DE: International Reading Association.

Barnes, D. (1992). *From communication to curriculum.* Portsmouth, NH: Boynton/Cook.

Brown, M. W. (1947). *Goodnight, moon.* New York: Harper & Row.

Bunting, E. (1988). *How many days to America? A Thanksgiving story.* New York: Clarion.

California State Department of Education. (1994). *The framework in focus: Answers to key questions about implementation of the English-language arts framework.* Sacramento, CA: Author.

Chamot, A., & O'Malley, M. (1987). The cognitive academic language learning approach: A bridge to the mainstream. *TESOL Quarterly, 21,* 227–249.

Cohen, E., & Gainer, R. (1995). *Art: Another language for learning.* (3rd ed.). Portsmouth, NH: Heinemann.

Cummins, J. (1981). The role of primary language development in promoting educational success for language minority students. In California State Department of Education, *Schooling and language minority students: A theoretical framework* (pp. 3–49). Los Angeles: Evaluation, Dissemination and Assessment Center/California State University.

Dudley-Marling, C., & Searle, D. (1991). *When students have time to talk.* Portsmouth, NH: Heinemann.

Ernst, K. (1994). *Picturing learning: Artists and writers in the classroom.* Portsmouth, NH: Heinemann.

Franklin, E. (1989). Encouraging and understanding the visual and written works of second-language children. In P. Rigg & V. Allen (Eds.), *When they don't all speak English: Integrating the ESL student into the regular classroom* (pp. 77–95). Urbana, IL: National Council of Teachers of English.

Gallas, K. (1994). *The languages of learning: How children talk, write, dance, draw, and sing their understanding of the world.* New York: Teachers College Press.

Graves, D. (1983). *Writing: Children and teachers at work.* Portsmouth, NH: Heinemann.

Harste, J., Short, K., & Burke, C. (1988) *Creating classrooms for authors: The reading-writing connection.* Portsmouth, NH: Heinemann.

Igoa, C. (1995). *The inner world of the immigrant child.* New York: St. Martin's Press.

Legarreta-Marcaida, D. (1981). Effective use of the primary language in the classroom. In *Schooling and language minority students: A theoretical framework* (pp. 83–116). Los Angeles: Evaluation, Dissemination and Assessment Center/California State University.

McGovern, A. (1969). *If you sailed on the Mayflower in 1620.* New York: Scholastic.

Mercado, C. (1991). Native and second language literacy: The promise of a new decade. In A. Ambert (Ed.), *Bilingual education and English as a second language: A research handbook 1988–1990* (pp. 171–195). New York: Garland.

Peregoy, S., & Boyle, O. (1997). *Reading, writing, and learning in ESL: A resource book for K–8 teachers.* (2nd ed.). New York: Longman.

Wells, G. (1990). Creating the conditions to encourage literate thinking. *Educational Leadership, 47,* 13–17.

Wong Fillmore, L. (1990). Latino families and the schools. In J. Cabello (Ed.), *California perspectives: An anthology from the immigrant students project.* San Francisco: California Tomorrow.

৯৯ Further Reading

Brookes, M. (1986). *Drawing with children.* New York: G.P. Putnam's Sons.

Hayes, C., Bahruth, R., & Kessler, C. (1991). *Literacy con cariño.* Portsmouth, NH: Heinemann.

Weed, K., & Ford, M. (1995). HELP: A holistic English literacy program for multilingual elementary classrooms. In L. Díaz-Rico & K. Weed (Eds.), *The crosscultural, language, and academic development handbook* (pp. 276–285). Needham Heights, MA: Allyn & Bacon.

Chapter

🌿5

Evaluating Reading, Valuing the Reader

Sarah Hudelson

Teaching from a whole language perspective makes sense to me. But how do I assess from this perspective?

How do I grade children if I'm not giving tests?

How do I work so that my evaluation of children better matches my philosophy of teaching and learning?

As an individual who works in teacher education in the United States, I frequently hear comments such as the ones I have just quoted, and I am aware of how educators struggle to change the ways in which children are evaluated. I know from reading and conversations that, around the world, educators struggling to teach from a more holistic view are engaged also in creating alternatives to traditional letter grades (Barrs, Ellis, Hester, & Thomas, 1989; Samway & McKeon, 1993). A major challenge for those working from a whole language perspective, then, is to bring assessments of children's learning more in line with teaching.

For many teachers, the most fundamental way to begin to achieve this goal involves not separating teaching and evaluating, but, rather, viewing them as two sides of the same coin (see, e.g., Genishi, 1993; Genishi & Dyson, 1984; Weaver, 1994). In operational terms, this means using children's processes and products to document their developing abilities, to record and describe their progress. This involves observing children as they work, interacting with them about their work, collecting samples of what they have done, and using these notes and products to describe them and their learning.

I would like to illustrate this approach to evaluation through the in-depth example of one child whom I will call Juanita. I worked with Juanita for 3 years as part of a research project in which I engaged with my colleague Irene Serna (see Hudelson & Serna, 1994, and Serna & Hudelson, 1993, for descriptions of the research). Specifically, I will focus on Juanita's development as a reader, first as a reader in Spanish and then later in English. My portrait of Juanita as a reader is based on my own and her teachers' written notes taken during instructional activities, notes from conversations I had with Juanita, and samples of entries from the literature response logs she kept as part of the reading and literature study groups in which she participated. I would claim that the picture that I am able to paint of Juanita presents a much more complete, complex, and detailed view of this child than grades on a report card could ever reveal.

℘ℛ Juanita's School

Before I share Juanita's journey to biliteracy, I need to provide some background information about the school she attended. The school in which Juanita was enrolled identified itself as one struggling to operate from a whole language philosophy, and the classrooms could be described as environments in which children became literate through engagement in reading and writing and through using spoken and written language to study content of importance to them. Books of various kinds (e.g., predictable, alphabet, poetry, picture books, novels, expository informational) were available for the children to use. Daily literacy events included teacher read alouds and discussion, independent reading of self-selected texts, minilessons on reading strategies for children who might benefit from such interactions, engagement in literature study, and utilization of books for investigating topics of interest. On a regular basis, children wrote for multiple purposes to different audiences. Learners also used theme cycles to identify and investigate topics of interest to them. (See the Altwerger & Flores, 1994, edited volume of *Primary Voices* for examples of how theme cycles are developed and carried out.)

Because many of the children in this school came from Spanish-speaking homes, the school supported an extensive bilingual program. In the bilingual classrooms, children who entered school more comfortable in Spanish than English began their formal literacy experiences in kindergarten in Spanish, and the program design called for work in Spanish to continue through third grade. As the children constructed their literacy in Spanish, the bilingual teachers also introduced books in English through read alouds. English language books were available for the children to examine. In addition, English language resources were available for theme cycle work.

When we began our research project, the teachers followed district requirements and issued formal, traditional report cards. However, they were already dissatisfied with the idea of using such symbols as *s+, s, i,* and *u* (satisfactory +, satisfactory, improvement shown, and unsatisfactory) to indicate how children were doing, and it became increasingly evident that the areas they were being asked to evaluate (e.g., in reading: sight words, knowledge of consonants, vowels and consonant clusters, word recognition skills, reading comprehension, performance on spelling tests, handwriting proficiency) did not reflect their beliefs about children's literacy learning. Many of the teachers became convinced that they needed to develop ways to document children's progress that were more in line with the ways that they were teaching (see Fournier, Lansdowne, Pastenes, Steen, & Hudelson, 1992, for a detailed description of how this was done in a bilingual second-grade class).

In grade-level clusters, the teachers developed check sheets that reflected the kinds of behaviors, strategies, and processes in which the children engaged. They also created forms on which they could record comments about children's participation in literacy events. They collected samples of children's work over time, and these documents became part of children's cumulative folders. Teachers used all of these sources of information about children to provide themselves, parents, and children with more complete pictures of their learning than that provided by report card grades. The portrait of Juanita that follows uses these sources as well as data I collected as I worked with Juanita for the 3 years.

❧ Juanita's Reading in First Grade

I met Juanita in first grade, her second year in this school's bilingual program. She had been in a half-day bilingual kindergarten the year before. At the beginning of first grade, unlike many of the other first graders, Juanita was already reading independently in Spanish. Her teacher's notes on Juanita's oral reading indicate that she was careful to sound out words; that she looked at the illustrations as she read, often commenting on them; and that she was able to retell the contents of books she had read. Her teacher once observed: "She reads everything in sight" (personal communication). My notes also indicate that many other children in the room saw Juanita as a good reader. During independent reading time, several of them often chose her as a reading partner. During daily choice or free time, Juanita could often be found reading Big Book versions of predictable books to small groups of children.

Beginning in January of first grade, the children began to keep a reading log, in which they recorded their responses to some of the books they were reading in groups and to some books that the teacher read aloud. Juanita's log responses confirmed both her enjoyment of reading and her ability to construct meaning. When, for example, she wrote about the picture book *El Nuevo Hogar de Greñas* (*Greñas's New House*) (Roa, n.d.), which is the story of a puppy removed from his original dog house to a new one that he refuses to accept, she noted:

Greñas estraño a su casa Y Greñas se escapo
A Mi Me Gusta ToDo El Libro

[Greñas missed his house and Greñas escaped
I like the whole book.]

She also illustrated her log entry with a detailed picture of a happy dog.

Her response to the book *Veo, veo. ¿Que veo?* (*I See, I See, What Do I See?)* (Kratky, 1990), which details a young reader's imagination as she examines various pictures, focused on one of the images in the book. After drawing her version of the illustration—a tree full of green foliage and two eyes peeking out—Juanita wrote:

A Mi Me Gusta cuanDo Dijo Son Los ojos de un cocodrilo

[I like when he said They are the eyes of a crocodile.]

By the middle of first grade, even though this was not the teacher's agenda, Juanita began to experiment with English reading. Her teacher's anecdotal records revealed that Juanita's experimentation began when she noticed that some of the beginner books that were available in the classroom in Spanish, such as translations of many of the Spot books, were also available in the classroom in English. When she discovered this fact, Juanita began to read the same books in both languages, reading these books first in Spanish and then in English. When I asked her about this, Juanita articulated her strategy for reading English as she told me that if she could read the book in Spanish first, it helped her read it in English. She also shared with me that she solicited assistance from home from both her mother and her older sister. Her mother would read a book with her in Spanish, and her sister would read with her in English.

By late in her first-grade year, Juanita also used her literature response journal to write about stories that she listened to in English. In response to Lionni's (1975) *In The Rabbit Garden,* for example, Juanita wrote:

A Mi Me Gusto cuanDo Los Conejo se Metieron en la Boco De La Bibora y sus Taron a El Zoro. La Bibora juga Ba co Los Conejos y Queria aser su amigo Les aYuDo a Que No Se Los CoMiera El Zoro

[I liked it when the rabbits jumped into the snake's mouth and scared the fox. The snake played with the rabbits and wanted to make friends. He helped them so that the fox would not eat them.]

In this example, Juanita made clear that she was able to construct meaning from the English language story, even though at this point in time in her L2 development she expressed her understanding in Spanish. By the end of first grade, Juanita had demonstrated that she was an enthusiastic reader who enjoyed sharing her enthusiasm with others. Juanita clearly was a child who enjoyed stories. Juanita had developed confidence in herself as a reader in her native language, a confidence that influenced her venturing into English. Juanita had figured out some strategies for becoming a reader in her L2, and she used both written material and human resources effectively as she worked to become biliterate.

⅋ఎ Juanita's Reading in Second Grade

In second grade, Juanita continued to read and write in Spanish, including participating in literature study groups in Spanish, and she also continued to read independently in English. Rather than allowing the children to choose the books they wanted to read and discuss in literature study groups (see Peterson & Eeds, 1990), the teacher assigned the children to particular books based on her judgment of their ability to read certain stories. At the conclusion of each study, the children evaluated their participation and wrote a response to the book. Juanita's teacher and the teacher assistant also kept notes on the participation of the children in each week's literature study, noting both how the children read orally and their contributions to the weekly discussions.

In addition to making comments that confirmed that Juanita read well orally, the adults' comments also revealed that Juanita transacted with stories in ways that went beyond retelling to include broader responses to literature (see Peterson & Eeds, 1990, for a discussion of these elements). Juanita frequently connected happenings in the books to her own life. When the children discussed Cano's (1986) funny story about a child's fear of what might be under his bed, *Que hay debajo de mi cama? (What's That Under my Bed?)*, for example, Juanita related her own story of being scared of something under her bed. After reading *Alexander que era rico el domingo pasado (Alexander Who Was Rich on*

Sunday) (Viorst, 1989), Juanita commented that she also had been blamed for something that she did not consider to be her fault (*A mi me hecharon la culpa cuando nos caímos en el lodo.* [They blamed me when we fell in the mud.])

Some of Juanita's comments had to do with the characters in certain stories. For example, she described the princess in the Spanish version of Munsch's (1980, 1991) *The Paper Bag Princess (La princesa vestida con una bolsa de papel)* as very smart because she made the dragon tired so that she could rescue Prince Ronaldo. In contrast, Juanita characterized the prince as *"inútil"* (useless).

She also made comments about what certain stories meant to her (the theme of a book). For example, she commented about the predictable book *Manzano, manzano (Apple Tree, Apple Tree)* (Blocksma, 1989): *"El arbol les dió a todos. Y al final tuvo un amigo."* (The apple tree gave [of itself] to everyone else. And finally it had a friend.) When she read the Spanish version of Fox's (1989) *Wilfred Gordon McDonald Partridge (Guillermo Jorge Manuel José)*, a story about a young boy's attempts to help an elderly woman regain her memory, she wrote about memory: *"Es lo que está en el corazón y es muy valioso"* (It's what's in the heart, and it is very valuable). And in response to a Spanish language version of *The Boy Who Cried Wolf* (Barnett, 1990), she noted: *"Con este libro aprendimos no desir mentiras"* (With this book we learned not to tell lies).

By January of second grade, her teacher noticed that Juanita was increasingly interested in reading books in English, as evidenced by a written comment in one of her December logs (*denos libros en ingles* [give us books in English]), so she invited Juanita to participate in both English and Spanish literature study groups weekly. As with the Spanish language books, the teacher and teacher's assistant chose the books children would read. Juanita was an enthusiastic member of the English language groups. She did not choose to write about her English reading, but she made numerous comments that were jotted down by the teacher. Often these comments reflected her careful examination of the illustrations. For example, when she discussed *Tikki Tikki Tembo* (Mosel, 1968), the predictable story about a young Chinese boy, she noted: "His hair goes up when he falls down," focusing on the picture of the protagonist falling into the well.

A favorite book was *Dr. DeSoto* (Steig, 1990), the story of a mouse who is a dentist and who foils a fox's plan to eat him while still caring for the fox's infected tooth; she offered these comments about the illustrations: "I like how he [Dr. DeSoto] has to go in their mouths; "There's steps for the big and little animals." Later, when we were talking about authors, she told me that her favorite book by Steig was *Dr. DeSoto*, and she provided a detailed retelling of the entire story with the book nowhere in sight.

By the end of second grade Juanita had become an effective reader in two languages, as well as someone who enjoyed reading in both languages. She responded to books often in terms of the meanings they held for her. She identified particular authors and books as ones she particularly liked. She attended closely to illustrations as well as to written words.

ᐧ᎒ Juanita's Reading in Third Grade

During her third-grade year, Juanita chose to participate almost exclusively in weekly literature studies in English. Every week the teacher introduced a number of books to the class, picture books and novels, written in both Spanish and English. After listening to these book talks, the children in the class chose the books they wanted to read and formed discussion groups for the books. The discussion groups were led by the teacher and an instructional assistant, both of whom were bilingual, and a Chapter One reading teacher and a special education teacher (also bilingual) who came into the room daily for literature study time (rather than pulling out certain children for services). At the conclusion of each literature study, the children wrote letters to the adult leading the study, responding in some way to the book that had just been read and discussed. Whichever adult had been involved in the literature study responded to the letter. The letter writing was a variation of the practice developed by Atwell (1986).

From the beginning of the third grade, Juanita wrote these letters (and everything else as well) almost exclusively in English. Because she had not written in English at all in second grade, I asked her about this recent development. Juanita explained that she had decided over the summer that she wanted to learn to write in English. Again, her strategy had been to turn to someone in her family for assistance. She asked her older brother to help her learn how to spell in English. She would spell words in English as best she could, and then he would correct them for her. After practicing over the summer, she was ready to write publicly in English in the school setting.

Over the course of the year, Juanita wrote more than 30 letters in response to books that she read. Taken together, they reveal that, as she had done in first and second grade but much more extensively, Juanita exhibited responses to literature that are similar to those documented by researchers who have examined talk in literature study groups, in both L1 and L2 settings (Eeds & Peterson, 1991; Eeds & Wells, 1989;

Peterson & Eeds, 1990; Samway et al., 1991; Samway & Whang, 1995; Urzua, 1993). Juanita

1. worked out her construction of the meaning of each piece of literature through her writing; this basic construction of meaning led her to recall specific aspects of stories that she had enjoyed, and it also included considering aspects of the books that were confusing to her

2. often connected pieces of literature to her own life experiences

3. often related one book to others she had listened to or read

4. gave some consideration to literary elements in the books such as character, central tension, and symbolism

5. gave specific attention to the language of the stories

I would like to use some examples from Juanita's letters to illustrate these points. The first letter I have chosen was written in October at the end of a literature study of a biography of Helen Keller (Markham, 1991). Juanita wrote the following:

> Dear Miss H_____
>
> Helen was very brave she med it in to she was eighty-seven. Miss H____ it was a little sad when Helen's teacher Annie died but wat I diren understand was that Helen alwis cicked and scrm screamded. It was very stranch when she got blind and deaf how did she got blind and deaf at the seem time whith chast a fever it was a rili stranch fever and she iven graduated from college and they named a bot after her they iven toled her to go see the president and everything helen did somthing very special whith her education she graduated from college she was very but very special for her family every time she got an invited everywher in the world she was very special to everyone she was very but very brave.
>
> Miss H____ I want you to bring out the book of Ramona Quimby age 8 or Charllet's WEb or Ramona and her father because I like reding fat books I tack ten fat book or 4 fat books out from the phoenix publick liberi I hab 4 books ot home from liberi and everytime I com from school I read oune

From her reading, it is clear that Juanita had developed a clear sense of Helen's life. She referred to many events in it, including how long Helen lived, her uncontrollable behavior, her graduation from college, and her worldwide travels. Juanita came away from this book with an admiration for Helen Keller the person, whom she characterized as "very but very brave" and "very special to everyone." Additionally, Juanita used her letter both to raise a question about something in the book that was not clear to her (How could a fever cause Helen to become both blind and deaf?), and to resolve this dilemma by deciding that it must have been a strange fever. Most probably Juanita's own experience of fevers had not been that they resulted in such serious consequences.

After responding to the book Juanita asked her teacher to bring out what Juanita referred to as "fat books," so that Juanita could challenge herself with these longer volumes.

At the end of November, Juanita wrote a letter in response to the historical novel *The Courage of Sarah Noble* (Dalgleish, 1991). The setting for this story is early 18th-century New England. A young Caucasian girl accompanies her father to the site of their new home in Connecticut and subsequently is looked after for several months by an American Indian family, while her father returns to their original homestead to bring back the entire family. When Sarah's family returns, Sarah leaves the Indian family but not without sadness because she has grown to care very much for tall John's family, and tall John's family has grown to care for her. In response to this book Juanita wrote:

> Dear Ms. B_____
>
> Sarah was very brave and she always said to her self "Keep up your courage Sarah Noble." Ms. B____I think it was sad when Sarah's dad came for her to teck her home and tall John the indian cam out and told Sarah "You go . . . Sarah . . ." then Sarah said "I must." I dot it was funny wen Sarah saw the indian children she was afraid.
>
> I dot the women she staid whith was mein to Sarah when she was ther.
>
> This book reminds me a little of the hundred dreses.
>
> Sarah liket her cap alot and slepet in it and at the end of the story she tock it oof and put it up.

Juanita's letter reflected the conflict within Sarah and tall John when she described her sadness at Sarah's departure, using the actual words from the book, "You go . . . Sarah" and Sarah's reply, "I must." Juanita also commented on the character of Sarah, characterizing her as brave and, again, using actual words from the story to justify her description. Additionally, in this letter, Juanita compared this book to another that she had read, *The Hundred Dresses* (Estes, 1974). In each of these books, a piece of clothing was important to the central character, as Juanita noted at the end of her response. Juanita thus reflected on the symbols in each of these stories, even though she did not use that particular term.

A book enjoyed by many children in this class in March was Dahl's (1988) *James and the Giant Peach.* Young James Henry Trotter lives with his two mean aunts, Spiker and Sponge. One day a little man gives him some green magic crystals that are supposed to help James escape from his sad life. But James accidentally drops the crystals at the base of an old peach tree in the yard. Magically, the peach on the tree begins to grow bigger and bigger until James can fit inside it. It is this peach that allows him to escape from the wicked aunts, as he snips it from the tree and rolls away inside it. As the story concludes, James shares the fruit of the giant peach with all of the children who ask for some, and he lives happily ever after inside the giant peach pit. Juanita responded to the book in this way:

> Dear Mrs. S_____,
>
> I like the part when aunt spiker and aunt sponge where singing the song that they adore themself and everything like that. What would of happend if the magic man didn't appear to James and James stayed with the aunts? I thought James was kind when the kids asked him if they could eat some of the peach and he just said "Of course you can everyone could have some!

Juanita obviously enjoyed the book and paid special attention to Dahl's use of language. Juanita cited specifically the dialogue that the two aunts engaged in, each telling the other how beautiful she was. Given that this conversation was set off from the rest of the page in italics and that it rhymed, it is quite understandable that Juanita would interpret it as a song. She also commented on James' character, again using specific language from the book to make her point. And, she invited her teacher to speculate with her on what would have happened to James if he had had to stay with his wicked aunts.

Beverly Cleary was an author that Juanita really enjoyed reading and having read aloud to her, and Ramona was a character she already knew. *Ramona and Her Father* (Cleary, 1990), which Juanita's group read late in April, focuses on what happens in the Quimby family when her father loses his job and is suddenly around the house a lot more than he used to be. Juanita shared this about the story:

> Dear Miss H_____,
>
> I thought Ramona was weird by putting on a crown of burs they cutted her hair I wouldn't of done that if I was her. I thought it was weird when Ramona was making a list of stuff that she want for Christmas if it was september. I think Ramona is weird her sister is always calling her a pest I wonder since she put that book Ramona the pest she started

calling her a pest. Miss H____I liked the part when Ramona was making sines that said no smoking smoking is bad and all like that she was really trying to have her dad not to smoke and at the end of chapter 4 the dad stoped smoking she put little scraps of paper in the cigerret box saying no smoking smoking is bad and she put posters in the curtains and everything.

It was not Mr. Quimby's plight as an unemployed person or the family's financial strain that struck Juanita. Rather she wrote about some of Ramona's actions, comparing what Ramona did to what she would or would not do in similar circumstances and deciding that Ramona sometimes acted weirdly. What appeared to be important to Juanita was relating personally to the character and recalling Ramona's successful efforts to stop her dad's smoking.

By the end of third grade, Juanita enjoyed reading novels and responding to them on multiple levels, much as adults in a reading club might do (Eeds & Hudelson, 1995). In addition, Juanita used writing as a vehicle both to reflect upon her reading and to engage with another person about a text. As I watched her choose novels during the school year, I wondered whether she ever still chose to read in Spanish. When I talked to her about this late in the spring, she told me that she was still reading in Spanish at home, even if she read more in English at school. She made weekly trips to the library with her mother, and she always checked out Spanish books. In the classroom, she did read a Spanish translation of Byars' (1981) novel, *Summer of the Swans*. She also shared her opinion that good readers could read in both English and Spanish. She said that she did not want to become like her older sister, who refused to acknowledge that she could speak or read Spanish.

৯ Conclusion

Juanita was the kind of successful reader all teachers would hope to have in their classes. She consistently received grades of s+ on district report cards, indicating that she was making and sustaining at least grade-level progress, both in terms of word recognition skills and comprehension. But the s+ designation does not begin to convey, to teachers, to parents, even to Juanita, her strengths, her developing abilities, her values, her individual personality as a reader. Such understanding of and appreciation for Juanita as an individual human being and as a learner becomes possible only through careful examination of her work and her participation in literacy events, her literacy products and processes, as documented by Juanita herself and the adults who worked with her. Such a careful examination reveals much about Juanita that letter grades do not.

Juanita enjoyed language and loved reading. She worked to become a more proficient reading by engaging in reading. She liked to share her responses to what she had read. She often responded to books by relating them to her own personal experiences. She demonstrated an interest in the characters in books she read. She had favorite authors and titles. She valued becoming biliterate, and she worked to make this happen. She developed reading strategies that were useful for her in both languages, and she made good use of them as she created meaning from what she read. She used resources around her to help her become biliterate. She was supported in her work by her family and teachers.

Some might argue that the picture of Juanita just painted is too subjective, not quantifiable, not reflective of where Juanita stands in terms either of other children or particular sets of objectives or standards. I would argue that this kind of detailed observation and documentation of children, and this utilization of children's processes and products, is precisely the kind of evaluation for which whole language professionals should be advocating and working to implement. A whole language philosophy of teaching and learning challenges us as teachers to reject traditional ways and means of evaluating children's language and literacy learning and to focus on the learners themselves, on what they are doing, saying, producing, and experiencing, on their struggles and accomplishments. In this way, literacy evaluation values children.

ᴘᴀ Suggestions for Teachers

1. Have a wide range of books available in your classroom, if possible, in children's native language(s) as well as English.

2. Provide time for children to respond to books using both spoken and written language.

3. Examine other teachers' ways of organizing and keeping observational and anecdotal records and experiment with ways of doing this for yourself.

4. Set aside time to observe children as they read and to take note of what they are doing.

✌ References

Altwerger, B., & Flores, B. (Eds.). (1994). *Primary Voices K–6: Issue on Theme Cycles.* (Available from National Council of Teachers of English, 1111 W. Kenyon Road, Urbana, IL 61801-1096 USA)

Atwell, N. (1986). *In the middle: Writing, reading and learning with adolescents.* Portsmouth, NH: Boynton Cook.

Barnett, C. (1990). *The boy who cried wolf.* Lincolnwood, IL: National Textbook Company.

Barrs, M., Ellis, S., Hester, H., & Thomas, A. (1989). *The primary language record: Handbook for teachers.* Portsmouth. NH: Heinemann.

Blocksma, M. (1989). *Manzano, manzano.* Carmel, CA: Hampton-Brown Books.

Byars, B. (1981). *Summer of the swans.* New York: Puffin Books.

Cano, I. (1986). *¿Qué hay debajo de mi cama?* Madrid, Spain: Ediciones SM.

Cleary, B. (1990). *Ramona and her father.* New York: Avon.

Dahl, R. (1988). *James and the giant peach.* New York: Puffin Books.

Dalgleish, A. (1991). *The courage of Sarah Noble.* New York: Aladdin Paperbacks/Simon & Schuster Children's Books.

Eeds, M., & Hudelson, S. (1995). Literature as foundation for personal and classroom life. *Primary Voices, 3*(2), 2–7.

Eeds, M., & Peterson, R. (1991). Teacher as curator: Learning to talk about literature. *The Reading Teacher, 45,* 118–126.

Eeds, M., & Wells, D. (1989). Grand conversations: An exploration of meaning construction in literature study groups. *Research in the Teaching of English, 23,* 4–29.

Estes, E. (1974). *The hundred dresses.* Orlando, FL: Harcourt Brace.

Fournier, J., Lansdowne, E., Pastenes, Z., Steen, P., & Hudelson, S. (1992). Learning with, about, and from children: Life in a bilingual second grade. In C. Genishi (Ed.), *Ways of assessing children and curriculum: Voices from the classroom.* New York: Teachers College Press.

Fox, M. (1989). *Wilfred Gordon McDonald Partridge.* New York: Miller-Kane.

Fox, M. (1989). *Guillermo Jorge Manuel José.* Caracas, Venezuela: Ediciones Ekare.

Genishi, C. (Ed.). (1993). *Ways of assessing children and curriculum: Voices from the classroom.* New York: Teachers College Press.

Genishi, C., & Dyson, A. (1984). *Language assessment with young children.* Norwood, NJ: Ablex.

Hudelson, S., & Serna, I. (1994). Beginning literacy in English is a whole language bilingual program. In A. Flurkey & R. Meyer (Eds.), *Under the whole language umbrella: Many cultures, many voices.* Urbana, IL: National Council of Teachers of English.

Kratky, L. (1990). *Veo, veo,¿qué veo?* Carmel, CA.: Hampton Brown.

Lionni, L. (1975). *In the rabbit garden.* New York: Pantheon.

Machlachan, P. (1989). *Arthur for the very first time.* New York: Harper Collins.

Markham, L. (1991). *Helen Keller.* New York: Franklin Watts.

Mosel, A. (1968). *Tikki Tikki Tembo*. Boston: Henry Holt.

Munsch, R. (1980). *The paper bag princess*. Toronto, Canada: Annick Press.

Munsch, R. (1991). *La princesa vestida con una bolsa de papel*. Toronto, Canada: Annick Press.

Peterson, R., & Eeds, M. (1990). *Grand conversations: Literature study groups in action*. Richmond Hill, Canada: Scholastic/TAB.

Roa, J. (n.d.). *El nuevo hogar de Greñas*. Mexico City, Mexico: Editorial Trillas.

Samway, K. D., Whang, G., Cade C., Gamil, M. Lubandina, M., & Phommachanh, K. (1991). Reading the skeleton, the heart, and the brain of a book: Students' perspectives on literature study circles. *The Reading Teacher, 45*, 196–205.

Samway, K., & McKeon, D. (Eds.). (1993). *Common threads of practice: Teaching English to children around the world*. Alexandria, VA: TESOL.

Samway, K., & Whang, G. (1995). *Literature study circles in a multicultural classroom*. York, ME: Stenhouse.

Serna, I., & Hudelson, S. (1993). Emergent literacy in a whole language bilingual program. In R. Donmoyer and R. Kos (Eds.), *At-risk students: Portraits, policies and programs*. Albany, NY: SUNY Press.

Steig, W. (1990). *Dr. DeSoto*. New York: Farrar, Strauss & Giroux.

Urzua, C. (1993). Faith in learners through literature study. *Language Arts, 69*, 492–501.

Viorst, J. (1989). *Alexander que era rico el domingo pasado*. New York: Simon & Schuster Children's Books.

Weaver, C. (1994). *Reading process and practice: From sociopsycholinguistics to whole language*. Portsmouth, NH: Heinemann.

❧ Further Reading

Goodman, K., Goodman, Y., & Hood, W. (Eds). (1989). *The whole language evaluation book*. Portsmouth, NH: Heinemann.

Graves, D., & Sunstein, P. (Eds.). *Portfolio portraits*. Portsmouth, NH: Heinemann.

Rhodes, L. (Ed.). (1993). *Literacy assessment: A handbook of instruments*. Portsmouth, NH: Heinemann.

Rhodes, L., & Shanklin, N. (1993). *Windows into literacy: Assessing learners K–8*. Portsmouth, NH: Heinemann.

Chapter

✂ 6

The Fiction Writing of Two Dakota Boys

Elizabeth Franklin

It is writing workshop time, the daily hour in which first graders at the Tate Topa Tribal School on the Spirit Lake Sioux reservation in North Dakota turn to their writing notebooks. These teacher-bound spiral booklets of 15 unlined pages, in which children can chose their own topics and genres to draw, dictate, and write, will ultimately account for more than half of all the children's writing this year.

Children I will call Richard and Jonathan sit side by side, as they often do, drawing pictures for which they will dictate texts. Richard industriously and painstakingly colors the sky blue behind a horse with long, horizontal strokes, then short ones as he turns the paper to fill in the spaces in the corners. Jonathan is intent on a muscle-bulging monster that he draws in one continuously outlining shape. He draws a smaller figure—"my bud"—to the side, and when the figure throws an egg at the monster, Jonathan goes back to the monster's face and adds a scribbled impact.

Across the room, Monica is drawing a princess in flowing dress and a conical Renaissance hat prior to beginning her romance. Next to her, Dawn eagerly opens one of the blank commercial note cards provided by a teacher and starts a note to Susan, three seats over, asking her to be her friend, while Susan is writing a note to her grandmother that she will deliver after school.

At the end of the hour, students will share their texts, and the two teachers collaborating this year on a research project will listen intently, observing and recording descriptions of student work as well as their own thoughts and reflections. Opportunity to write, choice in topic and genre for writing, and teachers' observations and reflections on those

95

choices are three important factors for learning to write in this bilingual-multicultural classroom.

As teachers in such classrooms, we are concerned with helping children expand their language proficiency, and we know some of the obstacles that stand in our way and in the children's way. Learning to write, especially for children growing up in bilingual-multicultural contexts who have been exposed to the genres and conventions of multiple literacies, is extremely complex. Much more is involved in learning to write than can be satisfied by instruction in standard orthography and English grammar. Such children face learning a method of communication and expression that is, as Himley (1991) argues, a "simultaneously cultural and expressive activity" (p. 8). Child writers bring themselves to the school task of writing, which means they bring themselves both personally and culturally, mediating their personal meanings by and through culturally appropriate oral/written genres and traditions. This view allows us to understand two reasons learning to write is so complex.

First, from the teacher's perspective, social institutions, and especially schools, do not value, utilize, or understand all the uses of language available in the cultures affecting their students (de la Luz Reyes, 1991; Dyson, 1993; Heath, 1983; Philips, 1983; Scollon & Scollon, 1981; Taylor & Dorsey-Gaines, 1988). Children who have preferences for and interests in particular genres and language styles may, in fact, have their language—and, thus, their meaning—rejected by the school (Dyson, 1993). Secondly, from the child writer's perspective, writing involves both the appropriation of, and the resistance to, certain meanings and forms. As Himley (1991) states:

> To learn to write, then, is not merely to acquire a new symbolic means for expressing one's private thoughts and ideas, but rather to learn about, to assimilate and come to own (or at least to rent) the very meanings one can have. It is also to fight other meanings, to resist, to want words but not finally to have them. (p. 98)

As beginning writers appropriate and assimilate certain genres, certain "performative" language styles, whether written or oral, and other uses of language in their pursuit of meaning, they demonstrate preferences for meanings they wish to explore and express (Bissex, 1980; Dyson, 1993; Franklin & Thompson, 1994). Beginning writers also resist meanings by not selecting other genres and features of language. The teacher is the closest professional adult to this complicated nexus where children negotiate meaning in a world of multiple literacies and, at times, of oppositional ones.

Providing children with numerous opportunities to write, as in the case of the writing workshop format, is an important first step. As they write, children will choose and explore particular genres, styles, and uses of language, involving themselves in an activity that is both culturally and personally expressive. The teacher, of course, is responsible for introducing other genres and types of writing that are deemed important for expressive development or the students have not yet experienced. But the teacher must also be able to notice and reflect on what young writers are doing as they write and illustrate in their chosen conventions.

These, then, are two assumptions:

1. It is important for teachers to observe and reflect on what children do in their production of written and visual works.

2. Children's choice of genres and styles reflects important personal and cultural interests that teachers can observe and reflect upon.

I would like to (a) develop these two assumptions a little more, prefaced by a context-setting description of the classroom, (b) briefly discuss the genres and stylistic choices of two Dakota 6-year-old boys within one particular classroom, and (c) give examples of the personal and cultural negotiation their writing illustrates.

✈ The Literacy Environment of the Classroom

On leave from my university position in 1993, I cotaught in one of the first-grade rooms at the Tate Topa Tribal School on a North Dakota Sioux reservation with Jackie Thompson, an enrolled member of the Turtle Mountain Band of Chippewa, who had been raised on the reservation and taught in its elementary school for 12 years. Tate Topa believes in a holistic approach to education (spiritual, intellectual, emotional, physical), and its mission statement emphasizes the importance of teaching to the individual child. In addition to the school's regular curriculum, children are taught Dakota language and culture through the Woonspe (Dakota for *wisdom*) program during and after school by various tribal elders and teachers.

The classroom's literacy environment emphasized thematic/multicultural instruction in which reading and writing were integrated into the content areas as well as in the use of reading and writing workshops. Some of these thematic units originated as teacher-chosen activities (e.g., Southwest Indian cultures), some as environmentally triggered activities (e.g., insects, after students had been catching grasshoppers on the grassy playground), and some as child-suggested themes (e.g., units on rodeo and ballet), all of which contained writing activities. In addition to content units and writing workshop, children also completed a variety of teacher-directed writing activities designed to introduce and deepen their understanding of specific topics and genres, such as written and visual responses to books, content-related informational writing (e.g., facts, reports), narratives (e.g., patterned books), letters, cards, and poetry.

Observing and Reflecting on Children's Work

Jackie and I set a goal of working with all the children equally, but we focused on seven of them for the purpose of piloting a child-study program, and we descriptively studied them in several ways. Daily, we listened as children discussed and shared their texts during writing workshop, and we recorded descriptions of and commentary about the texts and the child's process of creating texts, anecdotal records eventually consisting of 60–80 pages per child. At the end of each semester, the texts in each child's collection were categorized by type of writing activity (e.g., writing notebook, class books, responses to books), by genre (e.g., fictional narratives, personal narratives, informational writing), and by whether it was selected by the child or teacher.

The completed child studies, written collaboratively, opened with a lengthy observation of the child working on a project, followed by a summary of the parent interview responses, and a summary of the broad characteristics of the child's school learning. We discussed the written and visual texts by genre, described three to four themes from the works, and made recommendations for each child's continued learning. Each child study was about 100 pages long, including 50 pieces of work and numerous observation examples. They were read by a variety of other people, but readers normally included the child's parents/grandparents, a cultural leader from the Woonspe program, and an educational leader.

We would never have attempted examining students' work in this way without an understanding of and a belief in such an activity. An important aspect of all these studies is the descriptive-reflective process, adapted from that developed by Carini (1982) at the Prospect School, who provides both practical methods and theoretical support for this process.

First, we believed in the seriousness of children's productions, that they are not merely approximating some later correctness but that students actually do express important parts of themselves as person and learner. Carini (1982) argues that children create "works" as they write, draw, paint, play, and build. Creative works, whether of children or adults, manifest the individual in connection with cultural tradition and genres. These works are "semiotic spaces" (Himley, 1991, p. 5) in which the personal and the cultural are simultaneously negotiated. By describing and reflecting on these works, the adult teacher-researcher is connecting to, and connected with, the child's expressed meaning.

Secondly, an important practical method that Carini practices and advocates has been developed. The careful descriptive reading of children's works involves an initial viewing of collected works (e.g., texts and their illustrations) in their entirety for general impressions, followed by a detailed description of the content, style, images, and themes. As in the case of reader response to adult authors (Bleich, 1978; Rosenblatt, 1978), such a study of children's works normally takes place within a community of interested, involved readers/teachers who collaboratively create meaning as they read the children's works. In this process, one is not trying to be interpretively "right" about a work, nor is one judging it against outside standards. Instead, the teacher-researchers—reflecting, for example, on a child's narrative—"dwell" in the work in order to find, in Himley's (1991) words, the "shared territory" (p. 5) between the child and themselves. This is neither the reader's psychological intrusion into a child's work nor is it aimed at philosophical, or even pedagogical, certainty; it is acknowledged that ambiguous meanings will persist in this process and that meanings and understandings will change as the interpretive strengths of the teachers-researchers change (Carini, 1991).

Description and reflection, based on Carini's approach, is especially important for working with children from diverse social and cultural groups (Franklin & Thompson, 1994). This approach helps teachers and researchers (currently most of whom are European American) move beyond their perceptions of children as "acultural" (Dyson, 1993, p. 6) as they dwell in and share both individual and cultural meanings.

ᵝᐞ The Importance of Genre

We have realized for many years that learning to write involves much more than the conventions of turning speech into symbols through instruction in spelling, grammar, and mechanics. Writing is a particular kind of thinking, and different types of writing thus constitute, in one way or another, different types of thinking. This is true whether the types of writing are conceived of as the divisions of older tradition (description, narration, exposition, and argumentation); James Britton's three-part categorization (transactional, expressive, and poetic-fictive); or the differences between popular genres such as Monica's romance stories and Richard's adventure narratives.

Because of this, writing teachers pay attention to the issue of genre. Calkins (1991) recognizes its importance by presenting approaches to fiction, memoir, and nonfiction research. One of Graves (1994) "nudging" questions in a postwriting sharing session is to ask "Did anyone try a different form of writing today—a poem, a piece of fiction, or a personal narrative?" (p. 138). Clearly our goal as teachers helping students learn the powers of language is to introduce them to the different types; just as clearly, we can understand more about our students, and their writing expressiveness, by noting which genres they prefer or in which they seek to develop strengths.

This not always comfortable or familiar ground for the teacher, particularly in the genres of fiction. Although Graves (1994) admits that fiction is often students' favorite genre, he also claims it to be a "difficult assignment" (p. 287). Believing from his study of fiction that character is all, he views young children's stories as necessarily deficient because first and second graders only occasionally create new characters, preferring instead to use themselves or their friends as the main actors or using generic (or media-derived) characters such as Snoopy or the Ninja Turtles. But in that first-grade classroom, I was not as much concerned with helping children write "better" stories as I was with helping them write at all, and then seeking to understand their individual expressiveness.

The genre of adventure narrative is a case in point. Jonathan, Richard, and their other friends in the classroom sustained a strong interest in writing and illustrating this type of story throughout the year. Although it may seem close to "play" (e.g., writing about a fight instead of enacting it with toy figures), the adventure narrative contains both cultural and individual themes that the classroom teacher should be open to understanding. Cawelti (1976) argues that the adventure story, admittedly formulaic, is also

> the simplest and perhaps the oldest and widest in appeal of all story types. It can clearly be traced back to the myths and epics of earliest times and has been cultivated in some form or other by almost every human society. At least on the surface, the appeal of this form is obvious. It presents a character with whom the audience identifies, passing through the most frightening perils to achieve some triumph. (p. 40)

True to the genre as described by Cawelti, Jonathan's and Richard's "heroes" overcome obstacles and dangers while manifesting courage, strength, and resourcefulness. The subgenres of the boys' adventures—

combat, sports competition, the "wild west" and other situations—were closely associated with cultural themes and situations found in popular majority culture and with life on the reservation.

Dakota children, like most children in the United States, are exposed to movies, videos, books, and comic books from popular culture that feature the genre of contemporary adventure (e.g., James Bond, Indiana Jones, the Terminator, and Batman); however, they also hear many stories about the great Sioux warriors and leaders such as Sitting Bull and Crazy Horse, and they observe the honors given to veterans, particular Viet Nam veterans (often called "warriors" in ceremonies) who, dressed in combat gear, carry the U.S. flag during powwows. The adventure narrative, like all popular genres, provides a way of thinking about one aspect of human existence. When Dakota children write adventures, they experiment with what it means to be a hero, and they combine symbols, images, settings, and characters from their own, and popular mainstream, culture. As teachers, particularly of bilingual-multicultural learners, we need to be open to what this tells us.

Both Richard and Jonathan, the students to be discussed later, wrote adventure narratives and took advantage, in their individual ways, of the images and issues that genre allows. But many genre were present in the classroom, one of which was fantasy. Many Dakota first graders, including Jonathan, wrote fantasy narratives.

As with the adventure genre, teachers may at first look askance at fantasy because it can seem an escape from real life and from the responsibilities of "real" writing. But the children had heard stories read about unusual characters such as Amelia Bedelia and those in Dr. Seuss books, and they often watched cartoons and Disney movies or videos at home. This type of story has its roots in fairy tales, myths, and legends (Egoff, 1988; Jackson, 1981) belonging to a variety of cultures, and Dakota children are particularly familiar with many Dakota legends, including those involving the trickster, Iktomi. Let me add that these were taught, appropriately, by leaders of the Woonspe program and not as part of the classroom writing workshop.

As a genre, fantasy is a type of literature that focuses on particular themes and provides readers and writers a chance to explore issues that other genres do not. Fantasy, according to Yolen (1981), is a "story of magic" (p. 63), a "rehearsal for the reader for life as it should be lived" (p. 64), a "confrontation with . . . the great unknown that frightens us all" (p. 73). Although there are many ways to categorize contemporary fantasy, Huck's (1979) scheme includes: strange worlds and mythical kingdoms; animal fantasies; the worlds of toys, dolls, and little people; eccentric characters and preposterous situations; and magical and super-natural powers. Huck (1979) and others (Egoff, 1988; Jackson, 1981) also include some types of science fiction, ghost stories, and horror within the broad category of fantasy. In these settings and with these characters, child writers explore and challenge the socially organized and rule-governed "real world." In the process, they deepen their awareness of the magical, the fearful, the sacred, and the mysterious, while simultaneously confirming that which is most important in life. Fantasy and adventure narratives may overlap because many fantasy heroes encounter and overcome obstacles with courage and resourcefulness and adventure stories may contain fantasy figures such as robots and monsters. But fantasy narrative focus more on encountering the un-known, the mysterious and the magical, on experiencing boundaries different from those accepted as normal.

As with describing and reflecting on a child writer's adventure stories, the teacher encountering fantasy enters into a child's meaning-making regarding the themes and figures of that genre. The ability to shift gears and write in a variety of types of writing—poetic, informa-tional, fiction, personal, and the like—is the goal of writing instruction. As teachers of beginning writers, we must be aware of the types of writing our students choose, as well as be ready to offer other types by example or suggestion.

❧ Two Dakota Boys

Let me turn now to some brief examples of what I learned from examining the writing and art of first-grade children by focusing on Richard and Jonathan. There were many similarities between the two friends who sat side by side during writing workshop, offering ideas and help back and forth. They both knew some Dakota language and interacted regularly with a grandparent who spoke Dakota. Both good artists, they were also developmentally similar in their understanding of literacy. At the beginning of the year, both liked to listen to books but did not yet track when reading nor identify many letters of the alphabet. As the year progressed, so did their ability to retell books from memory, write their names, and do invented spelling. Affected by the culture of the school, by popular U.S. culture, and by the surrounding Dakota culture, both boys negotiated these cultural forces in beginning to learn to write through teacher-directed activities and their own self-chosen writing.

Richard and Jonathan produced approximately the same quantity of writing considering all activities (see Table 1). Both produced similar quantities of material in response to teacher-directed activities (i.e., all categories in Table 1 except "Notebooks"), and both utilized their

TABLE 1: TYPES OF CLASSROOM WRITING ACTIVITIES

	JONATHAN			RICHARD		
	No. Pages	No. Texts	%	No. Pages	No. Texts	%
Notebook	190		62	193		63
Response to Books	12	12	4	15	15	6
Theme Projects	7	7	2	6	6	2
Poetry	3	3	1	3	3	1
Group Books	7	7	2	7	7	2
Informational Writing	33	7	11	29	9	9
Narrative Writing	35	8	11	43	8	14
Letter/Cards	8	8	3	6	6	2
Annotations	2	2	1	2	2	1
Other	9	9	3	4	4	1
Total	306			308		

writing notebook about the same amount (62–63%) with similar material (one page long, written, dictated, drawn narratives of action scenes accompanied by an oral narrative). Although the two friends often supported each other's writing, their work reveals they were making individual choices about the meanings they wished to pursue as well as the genres that best helped them think about their ideas. These choices show two different individuals as they negotiate the worlds of meaning surrounding them.

Richard

Art was an important activity for Richard. He normally spent one entire writing workshop session on a single drawing and a written text, spending most of that time drawing. A writing teacher might have been frustrated at the amount of time taken, but it soon became clear the art process for Richard closely paralleled what has come to be called the writing process. Richard spent a long period of time drawing a specific feature, sometimes erasing things that were not as he wanted them, sometimes crossing out unsatisfactory details or whole pictures. Although he tended to draw action scenes in his notebook, he also drew single objects when he was learning "how" to draw a particular thing. Many pages in his notebook consisted of incomplete sketches, and often several pages of these "false starts" appear in a row in a his notebook, followed by the completed drawing. Through the process of drawing, and during the year, Richard taught himself how to "make things," and moved from simple, rounded bodies to more complexly drawn figures, from generic shapes of cars to the details of police cars and pickups pulling trailers. Acclaimed as an "artist" by other children in the classroom, Richard developed an increasingly sophisticated visual vocabulary.

In his notebook writing, Richard produced 117 narratives during the year, 60% of his total notebook pages (30% were art with no text, 5% involved "labeling," and 5% were classified as miscellaneous). Of Richard's narratives, 40 (34%) were personal narratives, and 77 (66%) were fictional. Most of Richard's narratives classified as personal came at the first half of the year; in the second half, he branched out into the world of make-believe fiction and stayed primarily in that genre. One observed difference in language development was that his early personal narratives involved much repetition; "I am playing" became a traditional start for Richard as he dictated or, later, wrote these personal stories, but that his later fictional narratives expanded the number of verbs dramatically, along with the number of different settings, characters, and actions.

One genre that particularly attracted him was the adventure story. Both Richard and Jonathan, along with their other friends in the classroom, sustained a strong interest in writing and illustrating adventure narratives, a genre discussed generally above. As I examined the works, they divided further into what I called competitive sports stories—which shared many features with the stories of other students in that genre and which space prohibits me from discussing—and combat adventure and western stories, all of which seemed to provide a more personal look into Richard's fictional writing world.

In his combat adventure narratives (four examples of which are in Table 2), the "good guys"—almost always Richard and other friends—fight unidentified enemy soldiers, cops, or generic "bad guys." For Richard, the use of the media-derived Terminator in 10/14 (Table 2) is unusual; most frequently, and importantly, he wrote of only human characters, resisting in his writing taking on the persona of a media figure. Cawelti (1976) points out that adventures may have either a superhuman or a human hero, and although Richard had an interest in adventure comic books, films, and videos, and although many of the boys actually "played Terminator" at recess, Richard almost always used human characters.

TABLE 2: COMBAT ADVENTURE NARRATIVES

JONATHAN	RICHARD
10/9: I was driving the smaller plane and I let three bombs drop. The army men blew up. My friend, Richard, jumped out of the happy face airplane. He grabbed on the ladder. He came up.	9/29: The cops picked us up. I shot my gun. The cops threw a fire bomb. They threw Clarence in jail. And I blew up the cop car. Clarence fell out. He had a parachute on.
12/3: Me and Richard are fighting the robot. The robot dropped the water. And Michael came and threw his numb chucks. The robot shot.	10/14: Me and Kevin shot Terminator. He shot me in the knee. We buried him in the ocean.
12/8: The bad guy shot Richard and me and Michael. I jumped out of the airplane and I shot the monster's head off.	12/4: I am flying a jet. Clarence threw a bomb at me. Smoke came out of the back. I crashed.
4/21: The bad guys came and they are fighting us. I blew them away. A robot jumped out. I knocked off his leg. And my bud threw an egg at his face.	3/29: A ship shot us and we fell into the water. We swam to the ship and killed the bad guys. Then we took off with their ship.

Art, as has been mentioned, played a significant role in Richard's writing, including the combat narratives. He explored various settings more than other writers in the classroom—struggles take place on land, in the water, and in the air—and he drew detailed vehicles such as helicopters and battleships on different visual planes in his illustrations. In fact, Richard systematically explored ways to draw jets, helicopters, and ships engaged in a variety of combat activities. Human figures occurred in the illustrations, but the focus was often on military machinery. A parent interview revealed that Richard's brother was in the Navy and that he read a variety of car and sea magazines at home.

Another type of adventure narrative for Richard was classified as "the western," a kind of story that may pose problems for American Indian children both because in mainstream formulaic fiction—and certainly fiction and films of the past—the bad guy is often American Indian and because the westward expansion tremendously affected the life and rights of indigenous peoples. On the other hand, the Dakota have been skilled horse riders for a long time, and many Dakota children still ride horses on farms and ranches as well as compete in and observe rodeo events. A rodeo is held in conjunction with each summer's powwow on the Spirit Lake reservation, and the children in the classroom played "horses" and "ranch" on a regular basis.

Although it may seem, in stereotype, to be a culturally inappropriate genre for such children, the western adventure story does provide them an opportunity to think about heroes who, with skill and courage, confront the natural forces of untamed animals or who, in a different setting than combat stories, confront the forces of evil.

In all, Richard wrote 26 narratives/illustrations and drew 13 additional pictures within the western theme, more than many other students (e.g., Jonathan wrote only two texts and produced two pictures of men riding horses). Table 3 contains five of Richard's stories of this type, the examples a rough approximate of his percentage of production of rodeo stories (10/4 and 12/10) and range material (sometimes combined with rodeo themes such as 2/1) in which a hero overcomes physical dangers and obstacles created by untamed animals and stories representing a "good/bad guy" theme (1/4), some with Native American perspectives (11/14).

TABLE 3: WESTERN ADVENTURE NARRATIVES

10/4: I rod the main bull. I won. My little brother is riding the horse. He has to chase the cow. It broke out of the fence.
11/14: I am riding a horse. I killed a buffalo. I saw a dog. And I saw tents burning.
12/10: I am bringing my horse to the rodeo to ride.
1/4: We're riding our horses. And we shot the bad guys. And Kevin's horse got shot. I had to carry him on my horse.
2/1: Me and Peter are climbing up a hill riding our horses. Then I saw a cow and we roped it. Peter shot one in the face. We took the cow to the barn. We brought it to the rodeo. And he bucked someone off and he almost died. He stepped all over him.

Several themes emerged from the descriptive study of Richard's written and visual works. His most extensive and important interest was the drawing and writing of action-packed adventure stories, both self- and friend-centered. A second theme in Richard's work, closely inter-twined with his love of adventure stories, was his love of machines, as mentioned in his texts and as painstakingly developed in his art work. Closely aligned with this activity was a third theme: Richard's sense of thoroughness, completion, and accuracy. These concerns were seen in the process of his art, in his ability and interest in accurately retelling stories, and in his attention, in other writing tasks, to follow the forms of different genres successfully.

Such an identification of student themes by a teacher points out strengths and celebrates the perspectives of the individual student. It can also point the way to what needs to be done for further learning. Richard's concern for thoroughness and accuracy, a personal strength in one way, also hindered his development in understanding the reading and writing process. His preference for order and accuracy became an area of vulnerability when learning to read and write because the most successful students are often those who can guess, take risks, and not have to understand everything about the system in order to engage in the activity.

Recommendations for Richard, based on the child-study, empha-sized a need for multiple reading strategies, including prediction-enhancing techniques such as cloze activities. Guided writing needed to be continued, and his interest in art and adventure fiction was identified as a growth-area; he needed to be helped to confront more complex issues in both his stories and drawings. Richard showed the ability to understand differences in genre form and content, and we recommended that he be exposed to a wider variety of genres and writing purposes.

Jonathan

In early May, the children were assigned "park murals," an art activity combined with reading (they had to follow written instructions). For a tree, Jonathan picked up a blue marker and drew from the bottom of the paper upward, making branches off the left side of the trunk with one continuous stroke as he moved upward, then crossing to the right side and down, making more or less symmetrical branches on that side before reaching the ground and adding buds and leaves. Four flowers were then produced in the same manner—stem, leaves, and flower petals with a single continuous line—and then following instructions, a butterfly on one flower and a park bench with three caterpillars. Given permission to add anything he wished, Jonathan drew a bunny on the ground, then a man coming down with a parachute. Announcing, "I'm going to draw an eagle," he did just that, finishing his rather unconventional park scene.

This classroom incident shows at least a couple of Jonathan's perspectives, once one came to know him. Art was an important expressive activity for him, as it was for Richard, but, unlike Richard, Jonathan was attracted to the combined themes of adventure and fantasy, as displayed in his additions to the park mural.

Jonathan took his art seriously. Like Richard, he sought to develop his visual vocabulary, progressing from the use of a single icon for many things (e.g., at the beginning of the year, he used a star shape to represent the sun, teepees, "numb chucks" [i.e., *nunchakus*, a type of fighting stick used in martial arts], and a helicopter's propellers) to more detailed or specific images. Furthermore, he insisted on having the time to draw, steadfastly refusing to move to writing/dictation until he was satisfied that the picture was finished. He often exhibited such a self-contained and absorbed mode of activity that both teachers sometimes felt as if they were genuinely "interrupting" him at his work when they gave further instructions. Some of this seriousness was also attached to his language. Jonathan told elaborate stories out loud as he drew, complete with sound effects. When it came time to dictate, Jonathan wanted the entire story recorded rather than a word or phrase, and he listened carefully to make sure I was being accurate. Once I mistakenly wrote *stopped* instead of *shot* as the last word in a dictation. I left the table to attend to something else, Jonathan persistently trailing behind me, repeating "No. You wrote it wrong. You wrote it wrong, teacher."

Jonathan's self-chosen additions to the park scene are an example of his flexibly nonrealistic bent, and he found many themes of interest in the fantasy mode. For example, in a teacher-directed assignment to create a serial sequence of actions following the days of the week, one illustration involved a bird, a broken or breaking egg, a toothy and mean-eyed monster of some sort, an almost table-shaped primitive animal that echoed the vertical shape of the monster, and several visual experiments such as a spiral flamelike design.

Like Richard, Jonathan appreciated the story form (of his narratives, 36% were personal—almost all done the first half of the year—and 64% were fictional). He also shared with his friend an appreciation for the genre of combat adventure (Table 2), and his narratives shared many characteristics regarding action and themes of conflict and victory. Jonathan was always a character, always a good guy, and the good guys always won. Usually it was Jonathan as person—and his friends—who attacked the bad guys bravely. His illustrations featured military vehicles as Richard's did—and action scenes where exhaust, fire, and bullets

TABLE 4: FANTASY NARRATIVES

12/2: Batman was going to my house and he saw my Christmas tree and I went outside and he saw me.
2/8: Tyrannosaurs Rex was crazy. Then he called out to his friends, "Look, I'm crazy."
2/22: I saw a little shrunk dinosaur. One with spikes. One with a long tail. I put them in a box and hid them.
2/22: I saw a horse and I stopped and I said, "Do you want to come with?" and he said, "Yes." It was Jamie with a gun. He called "hooray" and he could shoot down the sun from coming up.

whirled through the air (with sound effects accompanying the drawing)—but of the four stories in Table 2, two featured robots as characters and one a monster. Such humorous details as having his "bud" throw an egg at the robot's face (4/21, Table 2) were not uncommon in Jonathan's stories and always received laughs from the classroom audience.

Jonathan, finding the fantasy genre much more appealing than his friend Richard, drew six pictures of fantasy figures and wrote and illustrated 10 stories that we classified as fantasy (4 presented in Table 4). The plots are simple: Jonathan as a main character, alone or with a friend, interacts in some fashion with a fantasy figure. The human characters in his fantasies are not heroic, using strength and courage to overcome obstacles as in his adventures, but are primarily witnesses making observations of the presence of the fantasy element in real life. The suggestively mythic content of the final story (Table 4), with its detail of shooting down the sun, was reminiscent of the legend *Arrow to the Sun* (McDermott, 1974), which we read to children in class.

A final point is that Jonathan, for the most part, created original figures or transformed things into fantasy, rather than borrowing from children's literature or the popular media. Things discussed in class (e.g., dinosaurs) became part science and part fantasy in his written and visual work.

This tendency of Jonathan's was often seen in other classroom situations as he added his own interests to a learning activity. Drills (e.g., flash cards or worksheets) failed to hold his attention for very long but active engagement (e.g., putting the sentence strips of a poem in order) brought out his stamina. Often Jonathan would volunteer his own game-making abilities, turning math cubes into "robot fingers" and once making a number-matching activity into chutes at a rodeo. Jonathan frequently added his own touch.

In the Navajo unit, when the children were asked to draw a scene from the book, *The Old Hogan* (Garaway, 1986) (which Richard had done accurately, adding only a couple of details from Dakota life), Jonathan drew a hogan but insisted on adding Batman on top of it. In a similar activity, after listening to *The Star Maiden* (Esbensen, 1988), Jonathan drew the required scene, then added planets, a rocket, and a flying school bus.

In our summary of Jonathan, the image of storyteller came most strongly to mind. The theme of storytelling was not confined to his narratives but to his imagination-based play with classroom materials and his reconfigurations of classroom concepts into his own story-based perceptions. As only one example, after a classroom lesson on how apple trees grow from seeds, Jonathan drew and wrote a narrative about running to an apple tree, taking the apples off and eating them while taking the seeds out and planting them so the apples started growing again. Jonathan seemed at his best when thinking, writing, and drawing about imaginary or fantasy worlds, and one of our recommendations was that he be purposely exposed to fantasy and science fiction literature to promote his learning. Although the use of fantasy in simple first-grade narratives may seem to be unremarkable and indicate nothing individually about a student, in Jonathan's case it pointed to a major method of learning, an important way he had developed of appropriating scientific and cultural subject matter.

❧ Conclusion

I began with the contention that writing is a "simultaneously cultural and expressive activity" (Himley, 1991, p. 8) in which writers write through the language traditions and genres available to them in their cultures. Richard and Jonathan used narrative structures available in their culture, and the culture of the classroom, to think about ideas in writing and in art that were interesting and important to them. The full descriptions of the child-studies show the work of Jonathan and Richard to demonstrate that each boy was making definite choices about the type of narrative he wished to write.

Although the writing workshop activities were based on student choice, teacher-directed activities were involved with each child's interests in at least three ways. First, teacher units and themes introduced new images, symbols, and ideas so children were encouraged to think about a topic of interest in different ways or through a different perspective.

The reading of multicultural books about American Indians, in particular, was designed to present authentic images of Indian lifestyles and heroes, and a "rodeo" unit was developed to draw out student interest in that activity. It is, however, a complex process to understand how these images and symbols are used by children. Although it was an interest of Richard, the majority of children did not write western adventure narratives. For children like Monica (Franklin & Thompson, 1994), American Indian content was an important theme of her work, but other children fairly casually combined popular fiction features with traditional symbols.

Second, teacher-directed writing and reading activities provided new genres or brought known genres to children's attention. When letter and card writing was introduced, several of the girls quickly appropriated this form (and the materials provided), writing numerous messages to each other and to family members. Other children in the classroom were drawn to, and demonstrated a knowledge of, realistic fiction, romance, and horror, as well as writing personal narratives, poetry, letters and cards, and informational texts.

Third, children brought their own interests to teacher-directed writing activities, and it was possible, in the descriptive reflection, to discover the same themes and perspectives in teacher-directed work as in student-chosen work. For example, when children were asked, after hearing *Cookie's Week* (Ward, 1992), to retell a version based on their own lives, Jonathan related episodes about encountering Batman, mummies, ghosts, and animals who make a mess, whereas Richard related episodes about boxing, playing football, and hunting sharks. When children were asked to write "Once-upon-a-time" stories, Richard wrote about rodeos, and Jonathan wrote about ghosts and turtles. When asked to write a story using four sequenced pictures of snow scenes, Richard related a realistic story tied to the people and animals in the pictures, while Jonathan created a fantasy with trees and animals that turn colors.

Dakota children are growing up in a world with multiple languages, literacies, and cultures. They live in the world of childhood, with its primal appeal of adventure or fantasy or close relationships for survival in the natural and human world. They also live in a world heavily influenced by commercial entertainment whose fantasies and adventures both attract and challenge them. As well, they live in a world where the history of the 19th century and the reality of 20th are combined or conflicted almost every day. As they choose topics of interest for writing and develop skills in genres of preference, they begin to negotiate, both culturally and individually, the complex and often contradictory meanings of the textual worlds that surround them.

✒ Suggestions for Teachers

1. Collect samples of children's self-initiated writing. Categorize and describe the writing according to genre, theme, and style.

2. Collect samples of children's teacher-directed writing. Categorize and describe the writing according to genre, theme, and style. Compare the characteristics of teacher-directed writing to those of child-initiated writing.

3. Over an extended period of time, collect all the classroom writing samples of an individual child. After describing the writing, try to answer the following questions

   • With what genres does the child have experience?

   • In what genres is the child most experienced and most interested?

   • What children's authors might serve as good models to further the child's writing development?

4. After reading extensive amounts of multicultural children's literature to the class, notice how children's writing changes in response to this literature.

5. After collecting the writings of several children, describe differences that occur across children, with respect to their personal and cultural meanings.

✒ References

Bissex, G. (1980). *GNYS AT WRK: A child learns to write and read*. Cambridge, MA: Harvard University Press.

Bleich, D. (1978). *Subjective criticism*. Baltimore, MD: Johns Hopkins University Press.

Calkins, L. (1991). *Living between the lines*. Portsmouth, NH: Heinemann.

Carini, P. (1982). *The school lives of seven children: A five-year study*. Grand Forks, ND: North Dakota Study Group on Evaluation.

Carini, P. (1991, June). *Assessment: Another way of looking*. Paper presented at the seminar on Assessment: Another way of looking, University of North Dakota, Grand Forks.

Cawelti, J. (1976). *Adventure, mystery, and romance*. Chicago, IL: University of Chicago Press.

de la Luz Reyes, M. (1991). A process approach to literacy using dialogue journals and literature logs with second language learners. *Research in the Teaching of English, 25*, 291–313.

Dyson, A. (1993). *Social worlds of children learning to write in an urban primary school.* New York: Teachers College Press.

Egoff, S. (1988). *Worlds within: Children's fantasy from the middles ages to today.* Chicago: American Library Association.

Franklin, E., & Thompson, J. (1994). Describing students' collected works: Understanding American Indian children. *TESOL Quarterly, 28,* 489–506.

Graves, D. (1994). *A fresh look at writing.* Portsmouth, NH: Heinemann.

Heath, S. (1983). *Ways with words.* Cambridge, MA: Cambridge University Press.

Himley, M. (1991). *Shared territory: Understanding children's writing as works.* New York: Oxford University Press.

Huck, C. (1979). *Children's literature in the elementary school.* New York: Holt, Rinehart & Winston.

Jackson, R. (1981). *Fantasy: The literature of subversion.* New York: Methuen.

Phillips, S. (1983). *The invisible culture: Communication in classroom and community on the Warm Springs Reservation.* New York: Longman.

Rosenblatt, L. (1978). *The reader, the text, the poem.* Carbondale: Southern Illinois University Press.

Scollon, R., & Scollon, S. (1981). *Narrative, literacy and face in interethnic communication.* Norwood, NJ: Ablex.

Taylor, D., & Dorsey-Gaines, C. (1988). *Growing up literate: Learning from inner city families.* Portsmouth, NH: Heinemann.

Yolen, J. (1981). *Touch magic.* New York: Philomel Books.

৯ Further Reading

Goodman, Y., & Wilde, S. (1992). *Literacy events in a community of young writers.* New York: Teachers College Press.

Harris, V. (1993). *Teaching multicultural literature in grades K–8.* Norwood, NJ: Christopher-Gordon.

Hirschfelder, A., & Singer, B. (1992). *Rising voices: Writings of young Native Americans.* New York: Ivey Books.

McCarty, T. (1993). Language, literacy, and the image of the child in American Indian classrooms. *Language Arts, 70,* 182–192.

Chapter ৪ 7

A Bilingual Child's Choices and Voices: Lessons in Noticing, Listening, and Understanding

Mary Maguire

Dear Alicia. I have to tell you that I like Iran very much but I also miss Canada. I will be writing more about here later.

Dear Alicia Hello. I miss you so much every day. I miss you more and more. I hope that you are fine. My dad came home with a letter in his hand and suddenly he said tadaaaah! I opened it and read it. Thank you so much for your letters. I read the card and said: "I wish Alicia were here".

Dear Alicia my baby ducklings have turned into big ducklings. I had named them: margaret and lauwinnia. my chicks don't have names yet. By the way my parents got a house finally! Our house is not bad. It is quite big and it has a garden full of rasberry. Everyday I go in our garden and pick the rest of the raspberry.

Dear Alicia I really miss you so if you can Please send me your picture. I am going to send you my picture too! I have wrote a poem about Tulips

Dear Alicia I am going to send you my journals. Say Hellow to your husband for me
    Love Heddie

Dear Alicia
I have written an Iranian poem
    ps please send me back my journal when you are finished with it. Tank you.
    ps Please print my adress on the envelope when you right me letter. The postman here have problem reading cursive writing.

I begin with these excerpts from 8-year-old Heddie's letters to my research assistant, Alicia Romero. Heddie wrote these letters from Iran during a 6-month period following 4 years of English elementary school in Montreal, Quebec—a unilingual French province. These letters do not just convey information about her linguistic proficiency and expressive personality. They reflect Heddie's evaluative orientations as a writer and learner and her sense of self as a cultural agent (Moll & Dworin, 1996; Peirce, 1995). Her voice is clear as she articulates her particular situation at a given moment and specifies what she notices and understands to be possible. These letters, as well as the English and French texts she wrote in Grades 1–4, provide evidence that she can construct her own processes of understanding and valuing through dialogue with herself and others in more than one language.

Heddie's texts offer insights into her language learning in different contexts. Her discourse choices provide evidence that children's biliteracy accomplishments must be conceptualized as situated sociocultural conversations that vary across and within contexts. Bilingual children's conversations and texts offer insights into their abilities to construct their worlds as they notice, understand, and name them in their own process of self-definition (Maguire, 1989; 1994a; 1997). A bilingual child's sense of self develops through experience in concrete situations and in relation to others.

In this chapter, I focus on Heddie, a new arrival to the Canadian educational scene, to illustrate the inherent complexity of how languages mediate her sociocognitive and affective relationships with the world. Heddie was learning two mainstream languages at school (English and French) and two nonmainstream languages at home (Persian and Arabic). I illustrate, from her perspective, how these languages were personal and social systems and how she internalized and valued their different functions and social meanings (Bakhtin, 1986; Vygotsky, 1978). I examine how her conscious self emerges in a number of complex ways: through multiple discourses and languages imbued with the meaning and intentions of others, through her own active questioning and articulation of different cultural contexts, and through her sense making of her own biliteracy—or, more appropriately, multiliteracy. Because subtle shifts and slides of meaning collide, occur, and recur in children's situated literacy accomplishments (Maguire, 1997), biliteracy must be conceptualized as sociocultural mediated activities and social interactions.

❧ Establishing a Frame of Inquiry

Establishing a frame of inquiry for children's literacy accomplishments requires (a) beginning with children's voices as they access and appropriate multiple discourses and enact their preferred discourse choices in more than one language, and (b) assuming that the use of mediational tools (e.g., language) and mediating activities (e.g., journal writing) shapes children's literate actions and discourse choices in complex ways.

Becoming biliterate is a complex, dynamic, relational process. It is situated and distributed, constructed and negotiated. Biliteracy cannot be measured by tests, controlled by a teacher's practice exercises, or understood by mainstream researchers' tightly designed experiments. By listening to and talking with children about their own biliteracy, their thinking becomes more visible (Carini, 1979; Maguire, 1987). Traditional types of discursive practices are an insult to children's literacy accomplishments, the complexity of their thinking, representational abilities, and valuing.[1] Children's internalization of concepts and values about representational systems such as written language do not fit neatly into the regular pattern of a school calendar year nor into a researcher's short-term agenda.

Heddie is one of a group of 32 children my colleagues and I followed for 3 years in a federally funded project on minority language children's biliteracy and school success in dual track schools in two different Canadian cities, Ottawa and Montreal.[2] I focus here on how Heddie acquired the social practices that surround written language in different sociocultural and linguistic contexts and in two domains, home and school. Vygotsky's (1978) concept of learning as socioculturally mediated activity and Bakhtin's (1986) concept of language as involving dialogic relationships between and among multiple voices drive the theoretical framework for this inquiry.

Vygotsky (1978) emphasized the importance of written language as a cultural tool in young children's learning and language development. He argued that "human learning presupposes a specific social nature and a process by which children grow into the intellectual life of those around them" (p. 88). In Vygotsky's view, external social activity and personal psychological activity are mediated by cultural tools and practices such as reading and writing. Sociocultural approaches (Heath, 1983; Moll, 1990; Scribner & Cole, 1981; Vygotsky, 1978), derived from Vygotsky's concept of mediation have much to offer second language educators in establishing new frames of inquiry for teaching and learning. This is especially true with respect to explaining the sociocultural processes that influence minority language children's stances toward their own biliteracy in different contexts. Bakhtin (1986) maintained that a single text, utterance, story, or discourse can evoke varied sociocultural and linguistic environments, and he emphasized the role that social evaluations play in determining speakers' and writers' choices about, focus on, and self-regulation of knowledge.

Beginning with children's voices and discourse choices can be a powerful way to establish a frame of inquiry into their biliteracy and to understand who is actually mediating what for whom in what context (Maguire, 1994a, 1997). With respect to Heddie, her letters provide evidence to allow us to reject a deficit view of bilingualism and confirm that the myths Edelsky identified about bilingual children are indeed myths (Edelsky, 1986). Excerpts from Heddie's letters confirm that she is not language deprived; she is not insensitive to the task and audience demands of writing in particular contexts. She certainly views writing in different languages (e.g., English and Persian) as mediating tools and increasing her options for expression, communication, action, and reflection.

I have explored writing as a symbolic representational tool and activity and in terms of the functions it serves in the lives of bilingual children—from their viewpoints. I am convinced that children can be reliable and reflective informants with definite ideas about languages and how they are learning them, and the kinds of environments that enhance or constrain their biliteracy development (Maguire, 1987, 1989, 1994a, 1994b, 1997). Intertwined issues of choice and voice emerged in Heddie's reflections about her biliteracy her evaluative orientations and the interrelationships between her subjectivity and agency, identity and creativity. During the 4 years she attended English schools in Quebec, Heddie consistently announced herself to her teachers and to researchers in her classrooms. She consistently demonstrated her abilities to assess, voice, and reflect on her own literacy. She clearly articulated her memories of what she first noticed, her preferred discourse choices, and her awareness of her own personal agency in the different contexts in which she found herself. Take for example, her recollection of her early writing encounters as a new arrival in an English elementary school in a unilingual French province:

> I started writing in Pre K and I started reading in Grade 1. I started writing before I started reading. I would write said SED. I could read my writing. I spelled it the easy way but in the real books, it's spelled SAID. Miss R (grade 3 teacher) tells me what to write but most of the journal of grade one is about what I wanted to write myself. (Age 8)

Her reflective understanding suggests that her memories of these first encounters required both her attention to patterns and features of her language use and those of others, and her conscious awareness of her experiences and her own emergent sense-making abilities.

Heddie's comments about Miss R remind me of Vygotsky's (1978) evaluative injunctions about the function and organization of writing and teaching: "Writing should be meaningful for children, that an intrinsic need should be aroused in them and that writing should be incorporated into a task that is necessary and relevant for life" (pp. 117–118). He argues: "Teaching should be organized in such a way that reading and writing are necessary for something" (p. 118). In comparing her Grade 1 and Grade 3 teachers' approaches to writing, Heddie's evaluative criteria for developing her own textual power (Scholes, 1985) is clearly different from Miss R's (e.g., free choice vs. teacher-assigned topics), especially with respect to topic selection and control of written language.

Children experience biliteracy through an evaluative lens, and their engagement with the world involves their negotiation of an evaluative perspective. However, how children accomplish this is not addressed by second language acquisition (SLA) theorists (Lantolf & Appel, 1991; Maguire, 1994). Whether SLA researchers subscribe to Krashen's (1982) notion of *comprehensible input* or Swain's (1985) call for *pushed output,* they tend to ignore the more revealing evidence and understandings generated and valued by children themselves in natural settings. Either metaphor, input or output, suggests a digestive theory of language learning and overlooks the transforming potential of language use as situated human activity and ways of being in particular contexts.

ஒ Reformulating Beliefs About Biliteracy

In learning to read and write in any language, children make choices through which they construct definitions of themselves and their relations with their parents, teachers, and peers. These choices reflect their engagement with the world, self, and significant others. Previously, I defined biliteracy as all instances of communication and construction of meaning that occur in two or more languages around reading and writing and other symbolic systems (Maguire, 1994b). However, Heddie taught me that it means more than this. Noticing her appropriation of different discourse choices and voices forced me to re-evaluate my own beliefs about the teaching and learning of bilingual children. She taught me that biliteracy means access, agency, choice, and creation. She showed me how a child's diversity is distributed differently in different contexts with different interlocutors. She taught me to think of biliteracy as a fluid concept with constraints and possibilities (Bruner, 1986).

Although bilingual children have been observed by researchers, they, especially minority language children, are seldom interviewed or trusted to speak for themselves in mainstream research projects. Reenvisioning our beliefs about written language through children's voices results in a respect and support for children's diversity and an appreciation of the insights they can offer. It provides ways to modify and strengthen our own perspectives as educators and become learners once again.

Locating the situational contexts that mediated Heddie's literate actions helped me formulate three fundamental principles about children's biliteracy:

1. Biliteracy development is deeply rooted in sociocultural historical forces.

2. Children's emerging control of any symbolic system like written language is simultaneous with their active participation in cultural dialogues with significant others.

3. Children's cultural identities are socially derived, individually generated, enacted, and historically and politically situated.

The first principle necessitates viewing children as "speaking personalities" (Maguire, 1994a, p. 115) and their texts as "culturally expressive works" (Himley, 1991, p. 5), and both as historically situated in time and place. The second means understanding their texts (e.g., journals, letters, stories) not as an experiential add-on component in a school curriculum nor some task-object of study for a researcher's particular agenda or teacher's lesson (Lantolf & Appel, 1991). A task is always a social construction. Children's reconstructions of classroom tasks in their texts or conversations are active, generative, and intentional inquiries, though their interpretations may not always be in synchrony with their teacher's explicit articulation of classroom tasks. The third principle assumes that identity is a continuing social, cultural, and personal quest (Ferdman, 1990; Peirce, 1995). Understanding children's abilities to culturally position themselves in relation to multiple others resists linear ways of looking and appreciation for the intertwined intra- and interpersonal dimensions of their learning (Halliday, 1978).

How can this be done? Let's move to the nested contexts and textured layers of meanings embedded in Heddie's learning of four languages in different situations and the psychic space she perceives both the languages and situations offer for exploration, self-expression, self-regulation, and public and private recognition.

◈ The Nested Contexts of Heddie's Life

Bilingual children's literate actions are not givens. How and what they experience as literacy practices are not neutral political, cultural, or social phenomena. There is usually more than one context at a given time influencing children's generative, social, and cultural possibilities; cultural stances; and linguistic choices. To understand the nested contexts of Heddie's life, I began by adopting a sociocultural approach that includes three levels of study:

1. the broad social and institutional context that controls children's experiences of schooling

2. the social organization of classroom activities and how children's uses of literacy are distributed

3. the individual child as cultural agent and knower (Moll & Dworin, 1996)

I also began looking at Heddie from my own nested contexts as an Anglophone (English speaker) living in the predominately unilingual Francophone (French-speaking) province of Quebec and conducting research in dual track schools that serve Anglophone and Francophone communities. A common expectation for many Canadian and Montreal children is that their formal educational experience will be a biliterate one. Many Montreal schools also serve large Allophone (others) communities with varied sociocultural and linguistic populations. Children from these communities come to school with diverse cultural backgrounds and from homes where nonmainstream languages are used. Because of political legislation in Quebec, minority language children are obliged to attend French schools. However, a 5-year window in the language legislation, Bill 101, allows those parents who do not intend to stay in this unilingual French province to access the English public school system.

I have been able to examine the textured layers of meanings in Heddie's self-reported experiences and perceptions of reading and writing in more than one language during a 4-year period in two English-speaking schools in inner city Montreal. In retrospect, her personal testimony about learning more than one language helped me connect to the culturally expressive works I first noticed she constructed at Bridgeview Elementary, her first English school, and in other contexts.

Bridgeview has a strong reputation in the community as a site for inquiry and cultural dialogue (Bruner, 1986; Cochran-Smith & Lytle, 1993). This inner city, ethnically mixed, Montreal English school includes Chinese-, German-, Greek-, Ukrainian-, Dutch-, East Indian-, Bengali- and English-speaking children. They represent 23 different languages and countries. From the perspective of parents, especially new immigrants, this is a school that values diversity, encourages a cross-cultural perspective, and expects teachers to be thoroughly attuned with the children:

> It's the way they receive the children . . . . It's clear to me that the way the teachers treat the new students is good compared to my coun-try . . . . they try to understand the background of the children. Celebration of Ed Fitr (Iranian New Year) is good. These experiences expose the children to different kinds of countries and traditions and it makes then rich in their orientations.

> It was very good for us to see that in another country, we can express ourselves and our cultures and people want to learn about that.

> It's they way they (teachers) move with the children.

Children's mother tongue languages are valued alongside English and French, the school's official languages of instruction. Children are aware of the informal, enabling structures such as buddy systems that have been put in place to help new arrivals. They are aware of Bridgeview's encouragement of new friendships, intercultural relations, and invitations to share their cultural experiences and knowledge. Bridgeview also valued childrens' engagements with books and authentic literacy practices. For example, in Heddie's Grade 3 class, children had access to more than 1,000 English books and also to French books, though more limited. At the end of her first year at Bridgeview, Heddie offered the following advice on teaching a second language:

> I would have them (children learning a second language) look at books and . . . after they could read, I would tell them to look at all kinds of stories and then pick a little part of this story and a little part of that story. Like a girl that's ah named Rosie and a girl that's ah named, I don't know, whatever, and then they meet each other. It's like two books connecting each other so they have to use their imaginations. (Age 6)

After noticing this comment in a transcribed interview with Heddie, I began to listen more attentively to her voice. The depth of Heddie's explanations is a good example of children's voices helping us re-evaluate and confirm our own beliefs. For example, her advice reflects two theoretical concepts that frequently appear in current discourse on language and literacy: dialogue and intertextuality—the possibility to make connections among texts in varied contexts (Maguire, 1997). From an applied perspective, there was a noticeable effect on Heddie of being in a classroom that encourages and values children's oral and written expressions, explorations, and imaginations. In this particular Grade 1 English classroom, children did not do worksheets, did not have basal readers, and did not spend their time in English on fragmented literacy activities. ESL students like Heddie were not isolated from peers in pullout programs but were encouraged to make choices and develop their own textual powers (Scholes, 1985).

I first noticed the mediational potential of Heddie's biliteracy accomplishment in her texts because that is where I had first focused my attention. For example, in examining her English writing portfolio during Grades 1 and 2, she certainly provided textual evidence that she had internalized the social practice of using texts for different purposes. I sensed that her growth as a writer was occurring along many dimensions. I realized that writing in more than one language was more than just an internalization of social norms and control of written language conventions.

Noticeable features of Heddie's English writing emerged early in her texts. Her first journal entries in English demonstrated her ability to use a wide range of expressives (e.g., assertions, invitations, statements, explanations commentaries, apologies) to serve many functions (e.g., to signal an event that has happened, to refer to an object, to announce an anticipated event, to separate one genre from another, to signal to her teacher). Playing with language, intertextuality, and a sense of authorship began very early in her English journal writing (see Figure 1). Her Grade 1 and Grade 2 teacher, Miss Fraser, called this daily literacy event and teacher prepared booklet *Anything Goes.*

For Miss Fraser, *Anything Goes* simultaneously became both tool and activity for children's expressions. Heddie's varied discourse and genre choices suggested that she interpreted and used this mediating activity differently in different contexts. This was true for the children in the larger project. This also suggested that what may be conceived by a teacher as a fixed task, routine, or daily classroom ritual, may be perceived differently by children at different times for different reasons.

During 1992–1993, Heddie's texts were always accompanied by sparkly multicolored drawings elaborated in great detail and usually underscored some aspect of her written entry. By January of the first year, her first fictional narratives emerge as illustrated in the following excerpt (see Figure 2).

By midyear, she was able to report indirect discourse, and the first instances of character dialogue emerged. There seems to have been little doubt in her mind that she was the generator of these texts and that

FIGURE 1.

journal writing served different purposes on a given day (e.g., to inform and announce herself to her teacher, to connect to the books she was reading, or to use her imagination for her own creative and intellectual purposes). In Year 2, she continued to employ appropriately a range of

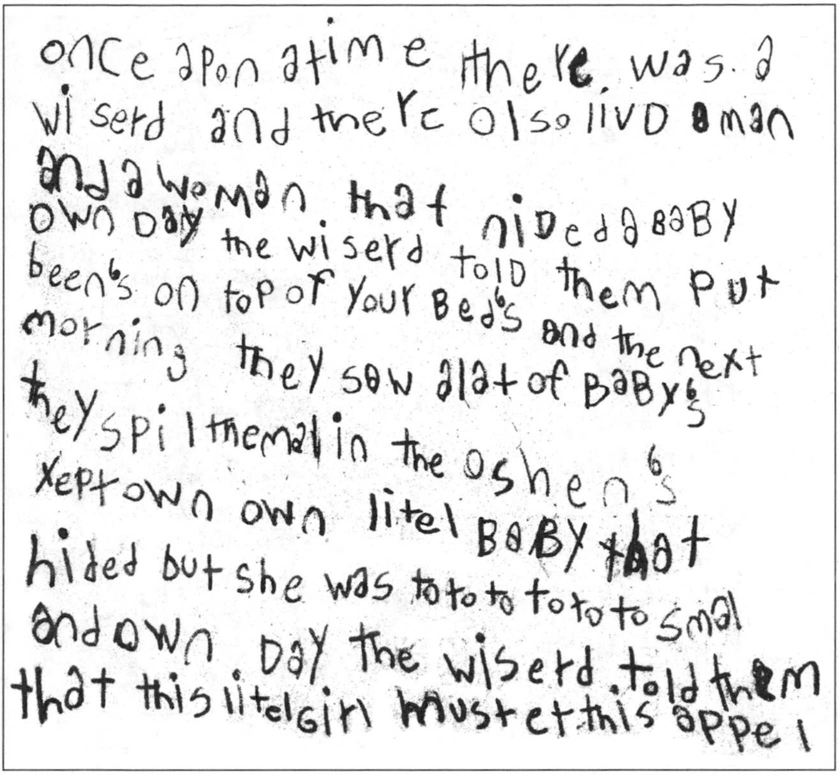

once apon atime there. was a
wiserd and there olso livD a man
and a woman that nided a baby
own Day the wiserd told them put
been's on top of your Bed's and the next
morning they sow a lat of BaBys
they spil them al in the oshen's
xept own own litel BaBy that
hided but she was to to to to to to smal
and own Day the wiserd told them
that this litel girl must et this appel

FIGURE 2.

temporal markers to order events in her narratives. She alternated
between using the present progressive to establish her presence in a text
to using the past tense to distance herself from the immediacy of a
situation. Causal relations continued to emerge as she expressed reasons
for or her feelings about an event. By the third year, she clearly names her
texts (see, e.g., Figure 3). In "Being Jelus," she reflected upon her feelings
about friendship and being jealous.

Although I noticed this affective dimension in her writing, I had not
clearly appreciated its significance in her appropriation of different
voices and discourse choices in the different languages and contexts in
which she lived and negotiated.

Heddie obviously knew that she had access to books, and had a
strong sense of what she was going to or could do. She made deliberate
discourse choices and explicitly signaled these choices to her teachers in
both languages (e.g., "Dear Miss Fraser I'm going to make . . ."; "*Alo
else, moi je . . .*"). Throughout the first year and subsequent grades, she

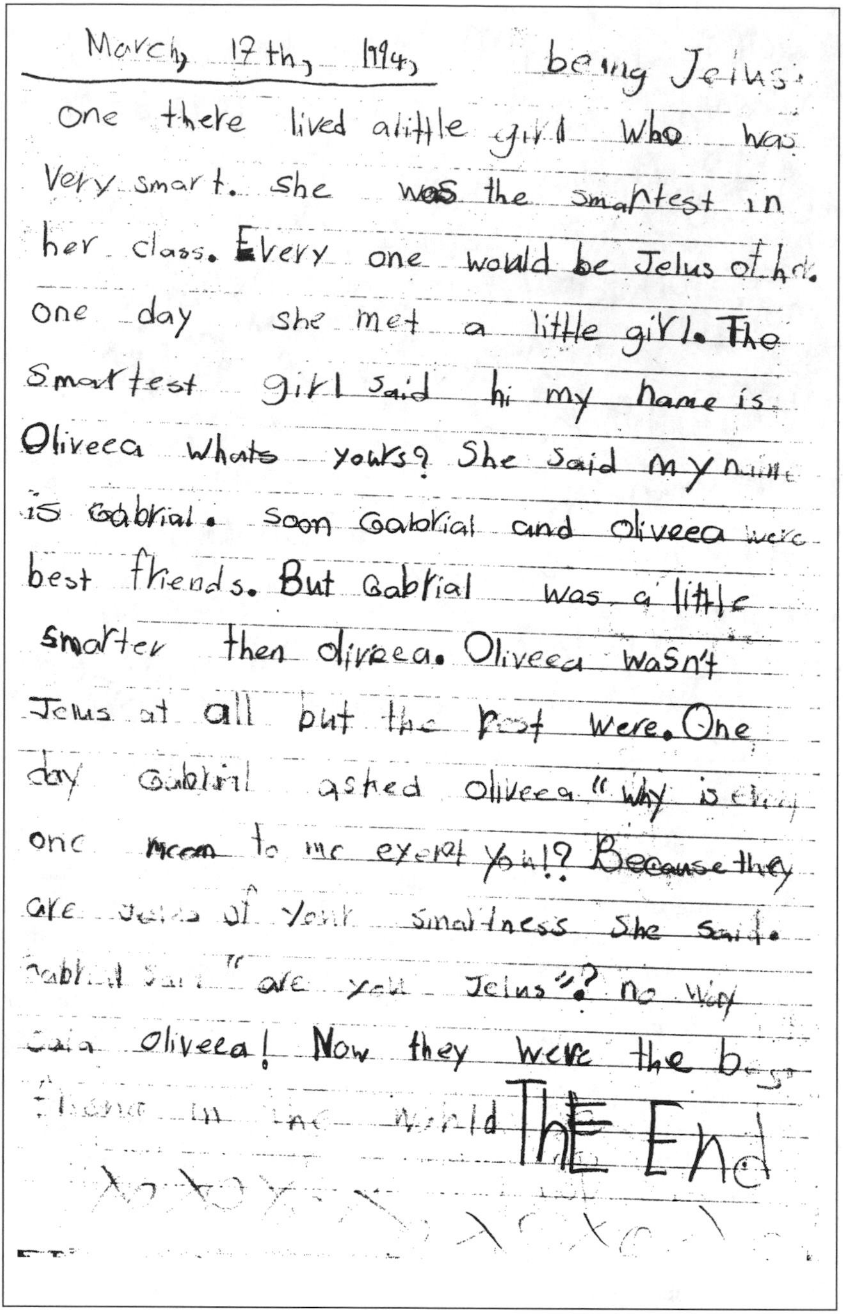

March 17th, 1994,   being Jelus.

One there lived a little girl who was very smart. She was the smartest in her class. Every one would be Jelus of hr. one day she met a little girl. The Smartest girl said hi my name is Oliveea whats yowrs? She said my name is Gabrial. soon Gabrial and Oliveea were best friends. But Gabrial was a little smarter then Oliveea. Oliveea wasn't Jelus at all but the rest were. One day Gabrial asked Oliveea "why is every one mean to me exept you!? Because they are Jelus of your smartness She said. Gabrial said " are you Jelus"? no way said Oliveea! Now they were the best friends in the world **THE End**

FIGURE 3.

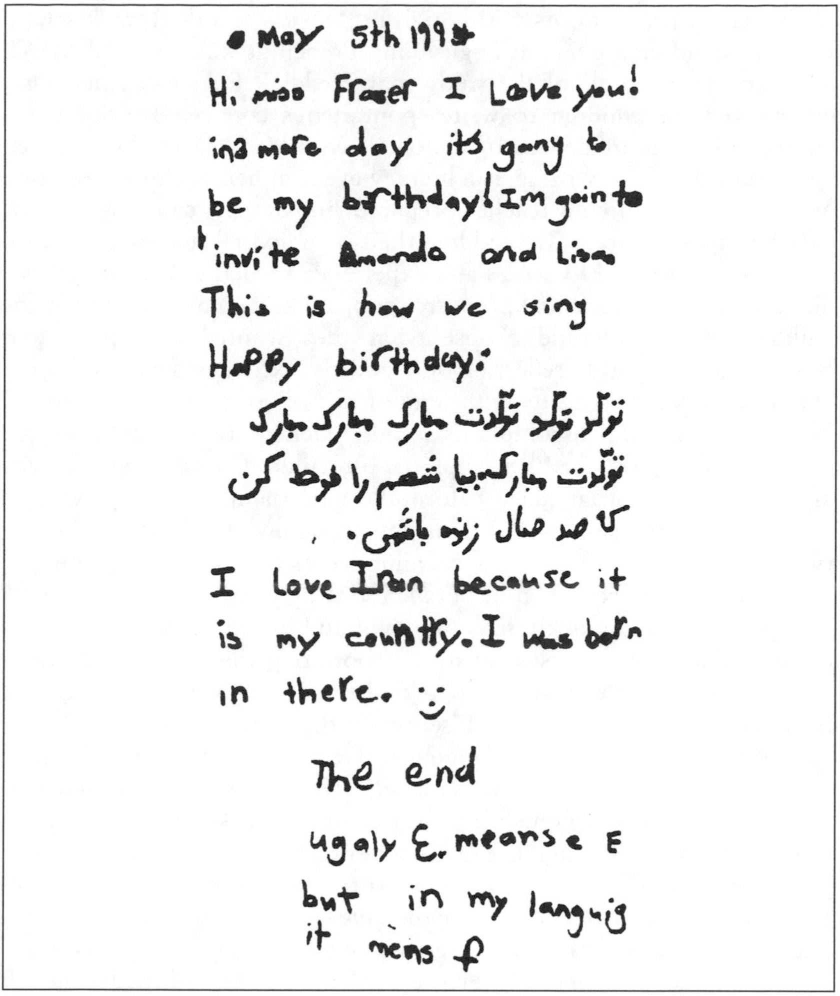
May 5th 199?
Hi miss Fraser I Love you!
ina more day its gony to
be my birthday! Im goin to
invite Amanda and Lisa
This is how we sing
Happy birthday:
تولد تولد تولدت مبارک مبارک
تولدت مبارک بیا شمع را فوت کن
که صد سال زنده باشی.
I Love Iran because it
is my country. I was born
in there. :)
The end
ugaly E. means e E
but in my languig
it mens ع

FIGURE 4.

included spontaneous minilessons on Persian for her teachers as illustrated below (see Figure 4).

Heddie's access to French written discourse was more limited. This in part may be attributed to a systemic institutional influence, that is, a program choice to offer a core French program of French instruction for 30 minutes a day rather than some form of an immersion program that theoretically could allow more sustained time and opportunity for writing (Genesee, 1987). However, Heddie's French teachers' beliefs about writing in a second language also constrained her access to and use of French written discourse. Although Bridgeview is a dual track school in which children are taught English and French, it was not until March 1993 of the first year of the study that Heddie's French teacher, Else, encouraged the children to write spontaneous connected written discourse in French. Influenced by dialogues with Heddie's English teacher, she included journal writing as a literacy event in her teaching repertoire and gave the children a teacher prepared booklet she called *Ma liberti* (My liberty). This tool gave children their own textual spaces to write on their own topics and to access and experience French written discourse. She called this activity *sujet libre* (free subject) and communicated to the children that they could choose what they wanted to express and represent in writing. In reflecting on Heddie's textual evidence and other children's accomplishments at the end of the school year, Else reassessed her own theoretical assumptions about teaching French as a second language. She questioned her emphasis on children developing accuracy and fluency in oral language before allowing them to attempt written language. Her decision provided insights into how Heddie was using the two languages consciously to access important resources for learning as illustrated in the texts from her French writing portfolio.

Heddie moved quickly from noticing and inventing certain features of the French language system to appropriating the discourse conventions of her French class. In spite of her seemingly limited language resources in French, she used Else as another interlocutor to help her create meaning in another language. Her same joyful and effusive personality (*"Alo Elce, Jedee Houra!"* [Hello Else, I said hurray]) surfaced in these first French textual explorations. As Else moved from distributing fill-in-the-blank exercise worksheets to adopting a whole language approach and providing opportunities for children's independent writing in French, so too, Heddie quickly moved from listing words and drawing pictures of their referents (Figure 5) to writing connected pieces of discourse in French (Figure 6). As in her English texts, she felt quite comfortable inserting Persian words or little lessons on the Persian language or Iranian culture in her French texts. By June, she was able to evaluate and express her feelings to her teacher about a critical incident that happened at school. By the fall of 1993, she was writing cohesive and coherent texts in spite of the limited opportunities her Grade 2 French teacher provided for writing.

Heddie provided textual evidence in English and French to reaffirm several Vygotskian principles:

1. Language is primarily social.
2. Language use is a symbolic representational activity.
3. Language is mediated by and through others.

FIGURE 5.

4. Language is a tool for sorting outs one's thoughts.

5. Language use is not constant across or within school and classroom contexts.

Two other important principles can be drawn from her evidence:

6. Just as the concept of a single definition of literacy must change to a plurality of literacies that vary in scope and dimension (Heath, 1983), the notion of a single language mediating children's thought and language must give way to new understandings of the roles that languages do and might play in their lives in different classrooms and communities.

7. The social abilities children need to become biliterate are those that allow them to engage in sustained, open-ended interactions that provide for authentic, dialogic encounters and their own textual explorations with self and others.

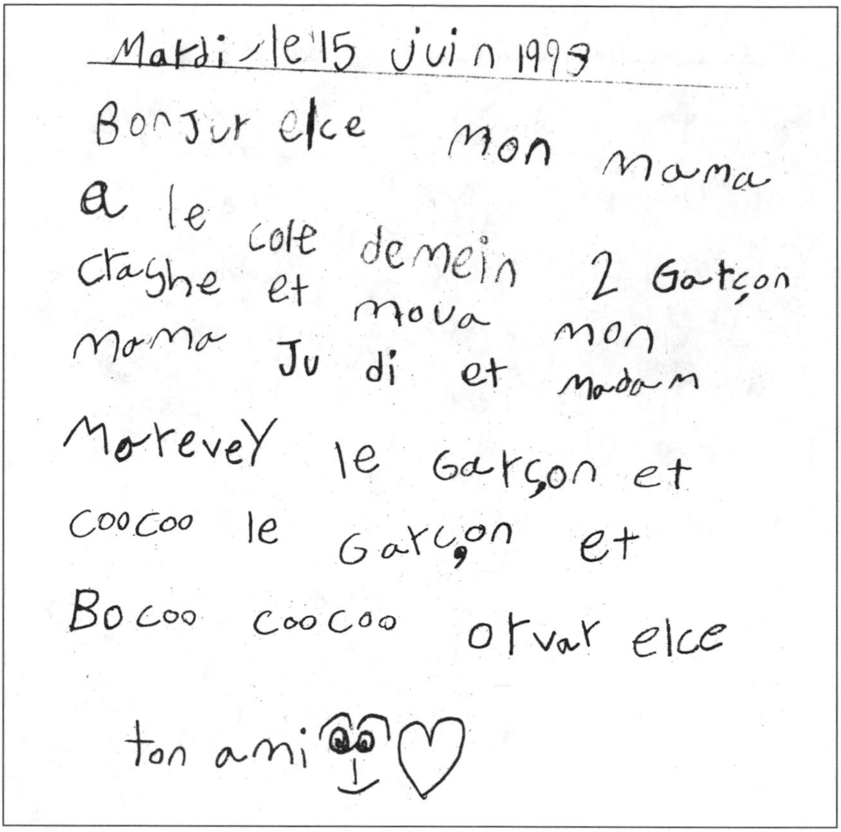

Mardi le 15 juin 1999

Bonjur elce mon mama
a le cole demein 2 Garçon
ctashe et noua mon
mama Ju di et madam
Morevey le Garçon et
coocoo le Garçon et
Bocoo coocoo orvar elce
ton ami ♡

FIGURE 6.

There is no doubt that Heddie's textual representations provided insights into her language learning in different classroom contexts. However, conversations with her at school and at home were central in understanding her understanding of the different contexts in which she thought she was expected to communicate, learn, and perform. In the next section, I focus on the importance of conversation as a research and teaching strategy in second language learning (Bakhtin, 1986; Maguire, 1994b, 1995). As Taylor (1993) argues, "it's the voices of children we want to hear but not in the echo of our own dried up abstractions" (p. 49).

ᵱᴀ Conversatons With Heddie About What She Remembered and Represented

Conversations with children in informal settings rather than structured interviews are more useful ways to gain insights into children's lives, their understandings of their situations, their cultural identities, and the textured layers of meanings in their symbolic representations in a first and second language (Maguire, 1987, 1997). Conversation is remembering as well as a process of engaging and negotiating values. The next series of excerpts from conversations with Heddie at home and school, when she was 8 and 10 years old, point to just how complex children's language learning is depending on the contexts. Her reflections about learning four languages in home and school contexts provide evidence that the boundaries between children and the actual cultural settings are not only bidirectional but also multidirectional (Himley, 1991). They challenge current theory in second language acquisition that tends to slot language learners into fossilized and dichotomized categories (e.g., first and second language, coordinate and compound bilingual), and characterizes them (and their language performance) as neat, definable and measurable types (e.g., *limited English proficient, fast* and *slow learners*) (Maguire, 1994a, 1997). They raise ethical issues about the use of treatment groups and ensuring equal opportunity for children's access to literacy practices and resources.

Heddie expresses an explicit fascination with the languages she is noticing, learning, and using in different contexts. English and French, the two mainstream languages that she is formally learning in school, do not have a close family resemblance (Wittgenstein, 1957) to Persian and Arabic, the two nonmainstream languages that she is informally learning at home. Heddie's comments are saturated with values and attitudes about her language learning in these different contexts. The depth of her comments point to the lessons we can learn from taking children's explanations seriously (Maguire, 1987; Zack, 1997):

Learning a Bit English . . . A very interesting language . . . I was very lonely

Heddie recounted her memories as a new arrival at Bridgeview Elementary. Conversations became windows on how she remembered her particular learning situations. She recalled her early experiences about "learning a bit English," her first social interactions, her appreciation of her kindergarten teacher's positive and sensitive response to her situation as a new arrival, and her feelings:

I remember that I was very lonely and that I didn't have any friends. I felt very sad because I found English a very interesting language and because I couldn't speak English I was quite sad. After um I learned a bit English, I was very happy then because . . . I thought English was a very good language and it is.

First I talked to Vahed and then I talked to Carmen. After I knew a bit English, only a bit English, I get, got friends with Carmen and she helped me on words, on lots of words and she really helped me. And that's how I learned English.

Mrs Aren (kindergarten teacher) was a very good teacher because whenever I had some snacks . . . she . . . and I was trying to say I have this for snack and I have that . . . I really wanted to say but I couldn't so she just held up my snack and for instance I got a banana and she said "this is a banana" and she wrote it on the board and that's how I got to learn English. She was very kind to me and whenever I felt a little lonely she tried her best to cheer me up.

In these excerpts, the role that social evaluations play in determining speakers' and writers' choices about and focus on knowledge becomes more obvious. She made explicit comments about the value of English as a language system and her first social interactions in English with other minority language children who helped her learn English. She assessed her kindergarten teacher's communicative orientation, demonstrations, and attitudes expressed toward her and in helping her learn English. They reflected her internalization of the different contexts of value and attitudes she sensed and noticed, experienced and negotiated. During the 3 years she attended Bridgeview school, Heddie presented herself as a child who believed in herself, had confidence in her abilities and ideas, knew that she was accepted and appreciated by her English teachers. She felt less confident with her French teachers and French classrooms where collisions between different intentions and values frequently occurred.

In March 1995, midway through Heddie's Grade 3 school year, she and her family moved back to Iran for 6 months where she attended school for a few weeks. In September 1995, the family moved back to Canada. During this 6-month period, Heddie wrote letters to research assistant Alicia Romero. However, upon her return to Canada, Heddie found herself in Grade 4, at Northpark school, an English elementary school in the west end of the city but within the same school district. Like Bridgeview, Northpark has a large multiethnic population but offers a French immersion program. In the following excerpts, she offers her comparative perspectives on the teaching and learning contexts at Bridgeview school and Northpark school:

In Bridgeview they (the teachers) were very kind. I wrote journals, Whenever I did a nice thing they would tell me and talk with me. In this school they say "Ha! nice work, next".

At Bridgeview, we celebrated holidays like Chinese New Year and Ed Fitr. In this school there's no Chinese New Year, no Iranian New Year. We get Christmas, Hannuka and a little of Valentine.

We are talking about sentences. Right now we are talking about nouns and verbs. We choose what we write in our journals but we got to choose more often at Bridgeview. I only write a journal here once a month.

I like it when they celebrate many things. Miss R [Grade 3 teacher at Bridgeview] wouldn't say if you didn't meet a deadline 'you are dead meat'.

If you know how to write a poem here it means nothing . . . they don't care.

I don't write stories here (Northpark).

In these excerpts, she contrasted the school and teacher discourse and literacy practices at Bridgeview and Northpark as enabling and disabling discourses that either did or did not support her personal discourse values. Noticeable here is her internalization of her teachers' different social attitudes toward languages and cultures. Heddie also demonstrated her competence in using different registers ("Ha! nice work, next"; "you are dead meat"). She considered the ethos of these two schools. She cherished her teachers' kindness, personal recognition, and celebration of cultural differences at Bridgeview and questioned her teacher's distant, perfunctory, and superficial acknowledgment of her culture and literacy accomplishments at Northpark. In this latter school, she did not feel noticed or feel that her efforts or culture were appreciated. She reflected on why she felt this way. She explained in the following excerpts from a conversation with her at the end of the school year:

H: the teacher wasn't so mean . . . but . . . she didn't ignore me all that much . . . . and in the end of the year I felt like . . . I was . . . keep on thinking to myself: Is it because of my teacher that I feel this way? Will I feel this way again next year? Or next year?

A: What do you mean by grade?

H: Like in the lower grades we used to do funner things just for the . . . being . . . you know younger . . . But I guess it was not . . . I was thinking . . . Was it the teacher's fault we didn't have all that fun or was it supposed to be that way?

H: . . . but they never let us write any stories. We did one journal in the whole entire school year. So one day a boy said: "Aren't we ever going to . . . to do another journal?" and the teacher said back: "Can't you see we're just too busy to write journals". It's like as if journals are something extra or something but they are fun . . . But journals are like part of writing I think and everything and part of learning . . . She just said: "Can't you see we're busy right now. We don't have time for journals". That's what she said back.

Evident in these excerpts are the tensions she sees between the discourses of schooling, her teacher's discourse, and her personal valuing of the discourses of stories, imagination, personal learning, and writing:

I had better learn a bit French . . . I am interested in French . . . if only I had . . . it's a nice class if only

Although English and French are taught in the majority of Canadian schools, the program configurations vary from province to province, school district to school district, and school to school. At Northpark school, Heddie was in a middle French immersion program (Genesee, 1987). Within this school district, French is taught for 30 minutes a day in Grades 1–3, in contrast to other school districts that offer early French immersion programs. In the following excerpts, Heddie reflected on and evaluated the learning and teaching contexts of her French language learning during a 3-year period:

I better learn a bit French so I can speak a little bit to him at least (Grade 1)

Like I write 2 pages of journal in French. I don't know why I can't speak French because I am interested in French but . . . I guess when I'm writing journal like . . . whenever I'm talking I'm a little too nervous so I cannot talk too much. (Grade 2)

But when I'm writing if I missed a letter or something so no one is going to read my writing yet. I write first and then I correct it. Well . . . not really correction well like maybe the spellings are a bit wrong. (Grade 2)

Miss J really tries to teach us. She really really tries . . . but she writes the word on the board and I copy it but I don't know what it means. (Grade 3)

If only we had a teacher like Miss R , then I think I would be better in French. (Grade 3)

I wrote a story about my birthday. I'm beginning to write a story about a little girl named Mary. She didn't want dolls. She wanted a bird . . . I lost my book . . . so I forgot where I was in my story. (Grade 3)

It's like, it's a nice class if only the boys don't ruin it because they, the girls are always nice. But the boys are silly. And it's always the boy's names on the blackboard, so if they would be good it would be better. And it's nice class. Like, I'm learning how to name the fruits and vegetables. (Grade 3)

I write poems in French at home. (Grade 4)

We had to write journals once a week of one page. You could write more but not less . . . about things that really happened. She really took French seriously. Like of any of the boys mess up she said if they said "who cares about French": "Well this is Quebec. You have to learn French so I'm just helping you learn. I'm not forcing you to learn French 'cause you're going to have a hard time living here if you don't know French." That what she told us all. (Grade 4)

She planned for us to write a page but the boys made so much noise she didn't have time so we wrote half a page (Grace 4)

Well . . . science because I understand everything he says in French (Grade 4)

Heddie's ambivalent attitudes toward learning French emerge in these comments. Although in Grade 1, she saw the need to learn French in order to talk with her cousin who lived in France, she was less confident about her speaking and writing in French than in English. She appeared to be less positive toward learning French in general as she moved up the grades at Bridgeview. During her first year at Bridgeview, she had a positive attitude toward French and claimed to be "interested in French." She attempted to make her joyful, expressive personality emerge in her journal *Ma liberti*. In her metadiscourse she signaled her intentions to her teacher (*"alo Elce mova ecrit"* [hello Else I go write]) and used the discourse conventions of many French immersion classrooms by addressing her French teacher by her first name.

However in Grades 2 and 3, Heddie was not impressed with her French classes, her French teachers, nor her learning in French. She attributed this problem in part to a small group of unruly boys who were routinely punished for their misdemeanors and a breakdown of the social order of her French classrooms. However, she still assumed some responsibility for her learning ("I lost my book . . . so I forgot where I was in my story"). Her equivocal attitude toward French may be attributed in part to her teachers' inexperience, lack of discipline and belief systems about how children learn a second language. They may also be attributed in part to her perception of her father's attitudes toward learning French. For example, she explained: "My dad said, It's better if you don't learn anything else but English and Persian. I don't talk French at home. I just know the names of the five fruits or something."

In March 1995, Heddie's parents decided to move back to Iran, where from their perspective at that time, French did not seem to have a necessary purpose in their lives. In conversations with Heddie just before the move she said: "We don't need French there. It's mostly English and Persian." Despite these constraints, Heddie did make progress in expressing herself in French during the 3 years at Bridgeview. Despite the classroom constraints that mediated what she could accomplish in writing in school, she knew she could deliberately exploit the symbolic potential of the French language system for her own creative endeavors, such as writing poems at home or school.

A subtle shift in Heddie's attitude toward learning French occurred when she returned to Canada and attended Grade 4 at Northpark school. Although there was more instructional time in French, the teaching of French at Northpark was quite traditional. The French teachers were very transmission oriented (Barnes, 1978) and spent most of their energies transmitting rules about language use to the children (e.g., *dictées*). Interestingly enough and puzzling to me, was the fact that Heddie seemed to have more positive attitudes toward learning French than in Grades 2 and 3. This may be attributed to a number of new factors in her life: Her family decided to stay in Canada for the next 3 years. Previously, her father had believed that too many languages would interfere in Heddie's learning; however, later interviews with the family indicated that he was "considering even placing her in a French school next year." Her mother was also currently learning French. When she first arrived, she focused on learning English. In a recent conversation, Heddie recalled that "at Bridgeview French was mostly about coloring. Here we have tests and quizzes. Tests are for the report cards and quizzes are to see if we are accurate. We get 20 words . . . ." She also stated that she wrote poetry in her French journal when she could.

Heddie continued to look at her French learning from a dual perspective—in terms of the school tasks she had to perform and the literacy activities like journal writing that offered her the freedom and agency to write poetry—her preferred medium. Despite the fact that she spent at least 50% of her school day learning in French, her general stance toward learning French in this school as reflected in her French school-type writing seemed less creative, less playful, and more serious than her Grade 1 French textual explorations. Her attitude was similar to the anxious tenor in her approach to learning Persian before she was about to return to Iran. Her concern then was about scoring well on the Iranian exam, a barometer her parents used while in Canada to ensure her reentry into the Iranian school system.

Heddie's pressure to achieve seems to have dampened some of the curiosity, critical thinking, and creative expression I noticed about her in the early grades. In a home interview, her parents expressed some concern about Northpark school, its emphasis on achievement and Heddie's anxiety about performing well there They were also intrigued by her poetry writing in French and Persian both at school and home and the psychic space both the languages and contexts seem to offer her. Her parents explained that writing poetry in Persian was not something they did at home, although Heddie's mother taught her Persian songs and poems.

Insights into Heddie's engagement with multiple languages and negotiating of different values also emerged in the home contexts in which she was learning Persian and Arabic. Although there is an Iranian school in Montreal that Heddie recalled attending for a few days when she first arrived in 1992, her parents chose to teach her Persian and Arabic at home. Heddie frequently declared her pride in her dual system of learning at home.

The following excerpts from conversations with her at home when she was 8 and 10 years old reflect her perceptions of the forms and functions these languages have played and continued to play in her daily life. They also reflect her ease in moving back forth between them.

> I like Persian . . . It's easy for me to write Persian . . . I never go from left to right . . . so it's not a problem having both languages at the same time (Grade 2)

> My father teaches me . . . I went to that (Iranian) school for week. I didn't really have fun the first few days because everyone made fun of me and called me a baby. "Hey a baby is starting grade 1 here". That's because they were 8 and I was only five.

> My Mom and Dad teach me everything; they're not real teachers like teachers that have been chosen teachers. (Grade 2)

> It's very easy for me to write Persian. I never did, never get mixed up once in English. Like I have Persian language and um . . . whenever I'm starting to write Persian I never go from left to right. So it's not a problem having both languages at the same time (Grade 2)

> Because in Iranian school that I went to for grade one here . . . for the exams, they never asked us to write stories. But I think if I write a story they won't say " Hey bad girl". They wouldn't punish me. They would just say "Yeah, Good but ah good". I think that what they want from us is to write journals about what has happened . . . not make believe stories . . . out of your imagination . . . they want to know us better. They want to know the family, the child. (Grade 2)

I like all of my lessons in Iranian. But I like science and the Koran the best . . . because I'm really interested in those two things. (Grade 3)

We have some tapes in Iranian and I really like them. Like for instance:
Recounts story in Persian first and then translates
There was this cow, this boy and he . . . They were a very poor family and they didn't have a Dad. The big giant ate the Dad and ah . . . It's a fun story and especially like the voices, because . . . Like the giant he has a wife and her voice is to so funny like whenever I'm listening to it. I keep on listening to it and it's so funny. The giant himself, himselfs voice is very terrible. And . . . Who would have such a voice? (Grade 3)

There's five books. One is science, one is the thing where you learn how to be family to God and there there is about family and then there's . . . you have to copy the little fun book and then the other is Math. Now Math, the letters, I mean the numbers are different but the signs are not different. The times is the same. (Grade 3)

I'm in grade three English and grade three Persian. (Grade 3)

I feel very good in Persian. I write poems in Persian (Grade 4)

Some of my memories are in Persian. Some are in English. I tried translating them into English but it doesn't work. They don't rhyme (Grade 4)

I like Persian study, science and history. I feel good in Persian (Grade 4)

Further glimpses into her home learning, uncover more subtle aspects of her language learning and different expectations and evaluative literacy orientations at work (e.g. ,"they wouldn't punish me . . . what they want from us is to write journals about what has happened . . . not make believe stories"). These excerpts, make noticeable her ability to handle many voices in both her real and fictional worlds and in different genres as well as make evaluative statements ("Hey bad girl"; "hey a baby is starting grade one here"; "her voice is so funny"; "himselfs voice is very terrible"; "who would have such a voice?"). She is certainly aware of multiple symbolic representational systems and can appropriate different voices and discourse norms.

All this complex language learning was acquired in natural contexts through authentic language use and meaningful talk within supportive networks of friends, families, peers, and some teachers. Heddie was very much aware of the norms, expectations, constraints, and possibilities of the different language contexts in which she functioned and lived. She articulated quite clearly the inherent values of the daily rituals and norms of different educational systems. For example, just before she was to return to Iran, she described the differences between her experiences in and expectations of the Canadian and Iranian school systems, as illustrated in the following comments:

> We wouldn't have reading and log in Persian because we have homework. (Grade 3)

> In Iran some of the teachers are a bit you know ah . . . not too generous. . . . I have heard though that the grade three teacher is very kind. (Grade 3)

> The biggest difference is the boys are separated from the girls. (Grade 3)

> I did not go to school in Iran because there was not kindergarten there although I could speak English when I was half of kindergarten here. (Grade 3)

> I usually get 20's. Twenty is a good mark (Grade 3)

She speaks in comparative terms of the task demands, gender differences, teacher ethos and differentiated nature of school tasks in different educational systems. She weighs her own performance in relation to institutional marks that indicate achievement norms in these systems. Always keeping a social radar for her teachers' personal attention toward her, she offers her assessment of the ethos of teachers in Iran. Getting and maintaining the 20s on the Iranian examinations was important for Heddie and her parents during their stay in Canada and certainly before they left for Iran: Her father frequently reported in conversations that "She always gets 20 after 20. She passed with an excellent exam." After they returned to Canada, there was less emphasis on getting 20s, although the Persian language was still maintained and used at home.

> I'm learning Arabic: . . . We have to memorize it because we need to learn the Koran . . . Arabic is the most difficult of the four languages

> . . . I write poetry in Persian

Heddie also offered evaluative commentary about her learning of Arabic and demonstrated her awareness of schools in both countries as institutional systems that apportion time to teaching more than one language for different purposes. She is conscious of the role that Arabic plays in her learning, daily life and creative endeavors and that symbolic representational systems can be different. In addition, she is also aware that movement between two languages is not a one to one matching exercise in translation and different written languages (e.g., Persian and Arabic) serve different functions and meanings in the home contexts (e.g., learning traditional school subjects such as science and math and Muslim religious traditions and beliefs) and require different literacy practices.

> I'm learning Arabic (Grade 2)
>
> Here, it's English and French. In Iran it's half Iranian and half Arabic because we need to learn the Koran. I know it. We have to memorize it. (Grade 3)
>
> Here there's English and French class and English most of the time. And there it's lots of time in Iranian and one and half of Arabic every day because we have to learn the Koran. I know three of them (prayers). Because it's just the beginning of my lessons. I know something in the Koran like Don't lie because you are going to be the enemy of God. (Grade 3)
>
> I liked reading my poems from the balcony in Iran. (Grades 3–4)
>
> My Dad give me homework everyday. I have to do it right Here. We learn about God. There's another book. It's not God's book but there's a book that we learn how to be nice to people. Then we get our book and we write handside (cursive). They say if you work, you get a nice return and if you don't and you're bad to people . . . . You go to hell. (Grade 3)
>
> There's five books. one is science, one is the thing where you learn how to be family to God and then there is about family and then there's . . . you have to copy the little fun book and then the other is Math. Math— the letters I mean the numbers are different but the signs are not different. The times is the same. (Grade 3)
>
> I write poetry in Persian here. Some of my memories are in Persian. Some are in English. I tried translating them into English but it doesn't work. They don't rhyme. You can't do it one to one. (Grade 4)

A year after her return to Canada, conversations with Heddie and her family indicated that she maintained a strong appreciation for and positive attitude toward her learning in Persian and Arabic: "I feel just fine in Persian. I like the Koran, I like Arabic. I like Persian study, science and history because I'm interested in those things." Her comments about learning Math in Persian and in English are intriguing: "I mean the numbers are different but the signs are not different. The times is the same." Her Persian texts and comments indicate that she is sorting out the equivalencies and differences between different representational systems along many dimensions at once in more than one language, more than one discourse and more than one context. Her texts and conversations indicate that she moves within multiple discourses that include a discourse of books, reading, writing and imagination; varied discourses of schooling at home, Bridgeview, and Northpark; in Canada and Iran; English and French teachers' school discourses; and family discourses that include culture, languages, religion, values, and encouragement of her accomplishments and Iranian cultural identity.

✌ Larger Contexts and Local Complexities

I have emphasized that Heddie attended English schools with a culturally diverse student population because within the political reality of Quebec's language legislation, which restricts new arrivals and immigrants from entering the English school system and regulates the languages of instruction in Quebec schools, Heddie normally would have attended a French school and been able to access formal instruction in English only in Grade 4. English is taught in French schools for approximately 90–120 minutes a week and emphasis is on oral rather than written language. Most French schools have *class d'accueil* (pull-out, welcoming transition classes to assimilate children into the Quebec language and culture) for new arrivals like Heddie to learn French. Her parents took advantage of the 5-year window in the language legislation: Immigrants who do not intend to remain in the province for more than 5 years can send their children to an English school. However, unlike the situation in some Ottawa English public schools, where newly arrived immigrants can expect formal, institutional support for ESL for their children, immigrant parents here cannot expect to have this enabling infrastructure in the Quebec English school system.

Heddie was not in any pull-out programs but learned and continued to use the two official languages within the natural contexts of her classrooms. These classrooms contained children from other nonmainstream languages and cultures as well as Anglophone children. They were not neutral learning environments and offered her different access to the two languages and discourse norms and, so, what she could accomplish in her own biliteracy (Maguire, 1994c). I have focused on the local complexities of Heddie's biliteracy (Street, 1995). However, I do not dismiss the fact that these larger political contexts that regulate the language of instruction in schools did not influence and play a mediating role in her literacy orientations, especially those she perceived that she could and should access.

I experienced initial difficulties in negotiating access to Bridgeview school from the school board, as far as I can ascertain, because I intended to study minority language children in an English school system in Quebec (Maguire, 1997). However, my research assistants' and my

first conversations with the school principal and teachers who participated in Year 1 of the project made it immediately apparent that at the
local level, Bridgeview as an inner city school was hospitable and open to
children, their families, and researchers.

There is no doubt that the principal, Mrs. Marana, played a strong
role in the positive ethos parents and children attribute to this school
that I described earlier, and in particular what Heddie perceived she
experienced there. Mrs. Marana commented that minority language
children at Bridgeview were doing quite well; this contrasted with much
of the reported literature on school performance of this population
(Gibson & Ogbu, 1991) and with our observations of other minority
language children. She provided a good example of what Taylor (1995)
calls an *advocacy model* of teaching, learning, and assessing what
children can and do know and mean. Mrs. Marana also provided a good
argument as to why teachers need to adopt an advocacy approach to
children's literacy profiles and creation of invitational literacy environments. Heddie's first Canadian classroom, from her perspective, was an
inviting place to be and become biliterate in school.

ɕ҉ Reflecting on Heddie's Voices and Choices

My inquiries into children's biliteracy began with rather naive questions
about school success and minority language students and a vague intent
to understand what combination of home and school factors enhance or
constrain their biliteracy. In this project, we spent most of our time the
first 2 years observing in classrooms and examining the children's written
texts rather than listening to children's and teacher's voices and choices.
Heddie forced me to make a methodological shift in my approach and
reformulate my beliefs in how children learn to write in more than one
language—that is, not only to notice what children are doing but to
listen to their voices as they explain, from their perspectives, how they
find their own expressions of meaning and inquiry in different contexts.
Children master sense and reference through socially available meanings
with others and their own social investment in everyday circumstances.
As I revisit the children's texts and learn more about the home contexts
of some of the children like Heddie, I sense a rich mixture of personal
values, lifestyles that resonates and that sometimes emerges in the
children's textual representations and voices in subtle and complex ways
(Maguire, 1997).

Adopting a respectful, reflective approach toward bilingual children
as many child advocates (Britton, 1992; Carini, 1979; Dyson, 1989;

Himley, 1991; Meek, 1991; Moll, 1990; Taylor, 1993) emphasize means being

- receptive to envisioning the explicit possibilities in bilingual children's situated literacy accomplishments
- alert to notice the implicit possibilities in bilingual children's actions, voices, reflections and textual expressions
- reflective rather than judgmental in our thinking about bilingual children's intellectual growth and mastery of the social meanings of thought—that is, languages

Home visits with children like Heddie revealed different and distinct communication patterns in terms of the languages their parents speak to each other, those in which they speak to their children, those they attempt to teach their children, and those children speak among themselves (Maguire, 1997). These parents were very eager to speak with us, initially in telephone conversations. We made it quite explicit that we wanted to discuss their experiences of schooling, their cultural values, their children's learning and cultural identities from their perspectives. Parents appreciated that our stance was as one parent put it: "to listen, understand and not to judge." This in turn helped us gain access to and better appreciate how a child's cultural identity is socially constructed and individually enacted.

For example, Heddie's strong cultural identity as an Iranian female and her self-confidence in approaching womanhood surfaced in conversations with her and her mother about wearing the Hijab. Her mother reported that she came from a family of seven girls and one boy and perceived that her father treated them all as equals. She encouraged this same sense of independence and self-respect in Heddie. "I like Heddie accept it (Hijab) herself." Her mother's subjective history conveys a sense of personal and cultural agency: "My sister doesn't wear it but I choose to wear it." She stated that she and her husband enjoyed their girls and believed that they were "somewhat different from other Iranian families "who pray just for boys" (Maguire, 1997). These comments better explain one of Heddie's Grade 2 journal entries as she writes about her own career possibilities:

> I would like to be an artist, a piano player, a sicolojist, an aesternot and a grade 6 teacher when I grow up. I got a sticker book from my Dad when I played one of the best paino players from Iran.

From Noticing and Listening to Understanding

From a traditional language perspective, the biggest difference among the first-, second-, and third-year journal entries was most apparent with respect to the increased repertoire of written genres and wider range of verbs and temporal markers and topics. Noticeable were the obvious signs of how Heddie's narrative writing increased in quantity and thematic and rhetorical complexity. The early narratives were frequently reworkings of stories she had heard or read (e.g., *Jack and the Beanstalk, The Little Mermaid,* and stories about princesses). She frequently included entries pertaining to religious events as well as descriptive pieces about events in her daily life, her culture, her language, and her country without being asked to do so. These were clearly her choices. Heddie was also aware of multiple types of language representations and the possibilities texts offered for representing her lived experiences and taking on of other voices (Bakhtin, 1986; Maguire, 1994a).

Heddie's journals frequently included many entries about her culture, her family, her languages, her country, and her own subjectivity in whatever contexts she found herself. For example, she expressed her ambivalence and nostalgia about leaving Canada this way:

> I really like my country, but I'm like I've really got used to here so I feel sad that I'm leaving here. So I am happy about going back but sad about leaving Canada. Iran is my first home and Canada's my second home . . . . Finding a house will take a long time. I'm going to live . . . well not live but stay with my grandparents for a month . . . so I get to study very well because there's a big exam.

Her strong identification with English and Persian continued in the letters she sent to us and to her best friend Sadda about her reentry to Iran and her Iranian school. When she returned to Montreal, we continued to observe her, learn from her, and listen to her articulate the sometimes contradictory and creative tensions in her language learning and her evaluative and fluid positioning of herself in different situations. In *Notebooks of the Mind*, Steiner (1985), writes:

> The processes of growth require resolution of the contradictory tensions between the social embeddedness of learning and the creative individual and drive toward personal voice. On the one hand to intensify and inquiry and develop a sense of commitment to a creative life, the learner needs models, teachers and collaborators. On the other hand, the individual while building upon the past needs to transform it and thus broaden his or her choices. (p. 208)

Children like Heddie and her classmates have forced me to consider new questions:

- What does it mean to become and be literate (biliterate) in classrooms and from whose perspectives?

- What constitutes a literate community in classrooms and schools and from whose perspectives?

- Who defines the norms for cultural and linguistic membership?

In a short but significant book, *How Texts Teach What Readers Learn*, Meek (1987) writes:

> If we want to see what lessons have been learned from the texts children read, we have to look at them in what they write. Of course, they draw on the whole of their culture, if we let them. We have to be alert to what comes from books as well as from life. (p. 38)

I return to my argument that children's literate actions are neither given nor neutral. Rather they reflect their evaluative orientations to the world, others, and self. They are situationally defined, negotiated, and constructed in and across the events and their lived experiences in their classrooms, families and communities. A fundamental result of listening to children's voices, noticing, and understanding their biliteracy over time is the development of a deep respect and support for diversity and appreciation of the diverse contexts in which bilingual children like Heddie live.

Vygotsky (1978) argues that "human learning presupposes a specific social nature and a process by which children grow into the intellectual life of those around them" (p. 88). Bakhtin (1986) argues that "A generative process can be grasped only with the aid of another generative process" (p. 102). Children's acts of meaning are intertwined complex acts of noticing, understanding and valuing. Hudelson (1984) argues that "allowing children access to their native language is one way of enabling those who have been silenced to speak" (p. 169). Listening to bilingual children's voices provides insights into their choices, how they are learning languages and negotiating their own evaluative orientations toward self, others, and the world. Internalization is not simply the transfer of concepts via language to the individual or the appropriation of social norms for acting and reflecting. Consciousness is more than awareness of one's cognitive and linguistic abilities. Listening to Heddie convinces me that no language test nor classroom observational check list could ever tap the nuanced language and meanings of her wondering, inquiring, conjecturing, considering, and imagining. Nor could they provide insights into the complexity of her learning, her creativity and her conscious sense of self. I end this chapter with her voice and discourse choice—a poem she wrote in Persian and translated into English:

درختان شونو پرز میوه در تابستان   دِگَر نوری نیست ـ از برق ـ و باران

شود پرز انگور درتابستان   دِگَر حبائی نئیت درغلامان

همه باز شونو مرغ و تمتّن   باوی، نوش، و رِّگار تَّر

اینها نشا نهایست ـ از لطف خدا   برای آرامش، و کاسایش ما

Talk to me world. Speak to me
So that I can make sense of the creatures, people and beasts
Live with you hop, jump and run
O huge world. Souvenir of very old times.

❧ Acknowledgments

I appreciate the sensitivity and understanding of Alicia Romero, research assistant and graduate student in the Department of Second Language Education, who conducted the majority of the home visits and established excellent cultural dialogues with the families. I also appreciate the help and openness of the principal and teachers of Bridgeview Elementary School in conducting this study.

❧ Suggestions for Teachers

To understand the contextualized complexities of differences and diversity, teachers may create different fora for conversation, consider the following assumptions, and choose appropriate ways to follow through.

1. Understanding the contexts and communities that mediate children's biliteracy and their literate actions assumes that everyone involved will discuss freely from a variety of perspectives. Teachers may want to form a study group and talk with parents and children about literacy practices in home and school.

2. To understand the intricate relationships between children's texts and their contexts is to appreciate the multiple nested

contexts that shape teaching and learning—interrelationships between intertexuality and intercontextuality. Teachers may want to hold focus group interviews with small groups of children (four or five) about their texts.

3. Children's literate actions must be seen as meaningful, purposeful inquiry not as an experiential add-on component in literacy curricula whatever the language. Teachers might want to observe children's literate actions in their classrooms and then ask them which literacy practices are most meaningful to them.

4. Looking, listening, and documenting are three fundamental ways in which we can become insiders into children's literacy networks and their contexts and understand them as socializers and symbolizers. Teachers might want to observe how children use different literacy networks inside and outside their classrooms.

5. Teachers' theoretical beliefs about language, language learning, literacy, and their own literacy practices provide different but not necessarily equal opportunity for children to engage in language learning and literacy as sociocultural, cognitive, and linguistic acts. Teachers might want to form a study group of fellow teachers and examine their own beliefs about language, literacy, and learning.

6. Despite the considerable time children spend learning a second language, they may not necessarily have sufficient opportunity to become biliterate and understand what they value about their own biliteracy. Teachers might want to ask children what they most value about literacy and what they think they are learning from different literacy practices.

ᑌᕽᐤ Notes

[1]*Discursive practice*: I use Schwandt's (1997) term to refer to particular ways of talking and writing about or performing one's practices that are coupled with particular social settings in which those ways of talking are regarded as understandable and more or less valuable. Discursive inquiry practices are at once ethical and political and not just technical undertakings.

[2]The larger study is supported by funds from the Social Science and Humanities Research Council of Canada (Grant No. 410-92-059): Biliteracy Development and School Success of Minority Language Children in Montreal and Ottawa. Principal investigator: Mary H. Maguire; coinvestigators: I. Pringle.

and R. Taaffe. It includes participant observations during 3 years in English and French classrooms, interviews with children, teachers, parents, and principals in four different schools as well as an analysis of children's written texts.

✌ References

Bakhtin, M. J. (1986). *Speech genres & other late essays*. C. Emerson, M. Holquist, V. W. McGee (Trans.). Austin: University of Texas Press.

Barnes, D. (1978). *From communication to curriculum*. London: Penguin.

Britton, J. (1992). *Language and learning*. (2nd ed.). Harmondsworth, England: Penguin.

Bruner, J. (1986). *Actual minds, possible worlds*. Cambridge, MA: Harvard University Press.

Carini, P. F. (1979). *The art of seeing and the visibility of person*. Grand Forks, ND: North Dakota Study Group on Evaluation.

Cochran-Smith, M., & Lytle, S. (1993). *Inside outside: Teachers, research and knowledge*. New York: Teachers College Press.

Dyson, A. H. (1989). *Multiple worlds of child writers: Friends learning to write*. New York: Teachers College Press.

Edelsky, C. (1986). *Writing in a bilingual program: Habia una vez*. Norwood, NJ: Ablex.

Ferdman, B. (1990). Literacy and cultural identity. *Harvard Educational Review, 60*, 181–204.

Genesee, F. (1987). *Learning through two languages: Studies of immersion and bilingual education*. New York: Newbury House.

Gibson, M., & Ogbu, J. (Eds.) (1991). *Minority status and schooling: A comparative study of immigrant and involuntary minorities*. New York: Garland.

Halliday, M. A. K. (1978). *Language as social semiotic: The social interpretation of language and meaning*. Baltimore, MD: University Park Press.

Heath, S. B. (1983). *Ways with words*. Cambridge, MA: Cambridge University Press.

Himley, M. (1991). *Shared territory: Understanding children's writing as works*. New York: Oxford University Press.

Hudelson, S. (1984). Kan yu ret and rayt in ingles: Children become literate in English as a second language. *TESOL Quarterly, 18*, 221–238.

Krashen, S. (1982). *Principles and practices in second language acquisition*. New York: Pergamon Press.

Lantolf, J., & Appel, G. (Eds.). Vygotskian approaches to second language research (pp. 1–32). Cambridge, MA: Cambridge University Press.

Maguire, M. H. (1987). Is writing a story that more complex in a second language than in a first language: Children's perceptions. *Carleton Papers in Applied Language Study, 4*, 17–65.

Maguire, M. H. (1989). *Middle grade French immersion children's perceptions and productions of English and French written narratives*. Unpublished doctoral dissertation.

Maguire, M. H. (1994a). Cultural stances of two Quebec bilingual children informing storytelling. *Comparative Education Review, 38,* 115–144.

Maguire, M. H. (1994b). Getting beyond instructional time and program type in second language teaching and learning. *Journal of the Canadian Association of Applied Linguistics, 11*(2), 29–50.

Maguire, M. H. (1994c). Engaging children in language and learning in the primary school: Experiencing, enquiring, examining. In M. C. Courtland & T. J. Gambel (Eds.), *Curriculum planning in the language arts K–12: An holistic perspective* (pp. 70–104). North York, Canada: Captus Press.

Maguire, M. H. (Ed.). (1995). *Dialogue in a major key: Women scholars speak.* Urbana, IL: National Council of Teachers of English.

Maguire, M. H. (1997). Shared and negotiated territories; The socio-cultural embeddedness of children's acts of meaning. In A. Pollard, D. Thiessen, & A. Filer (Eds.), *Children and their curriculum: The perspectives of primary and elementary school children* (pp. 51–80). London: Falmer Press.

Meek, M. (1987). *How texts teach what readers learn.* London: The Thimble Press.

Meek, M. (1991). *On being literate.* London: The Bodley Head.

Moll, L. C. (Ed.). (1990). *Vygotsky and education: Instructional implications and applications of sociohistorical psychology.* New York: Cambridge University Press.

Moll, L. C., & Dworin, J. E. (1996). Biliteracy development in classrooms: Social dynamics and cultural possibilities. In D. Nicks (Ed.), *Child discourse and learning* (pp. 221–245). Cambridge: University of Cambridge.

Peirce, B. N. (1995). Social identity, investment and language learning. *TESOL Quarterly, 29,* 9–31.

Scholes, R. (1985). *Textual power: Literary theory and the teaching of English.* New Haven, CT: Yale University Press.

Scribner, S., & Cole, M. (1981). *The psychology of literacy.* Cambridge, MA: Harvard University Press.

Steiner, V. J. (1985) *Notebooks of the mind: Explorations of teaching.* New York: Haysen & Raw.

Street, B. V. (1995). *Social literacies: Critical approaches to literacy in development, ethnography and education.* New York: Longman.

Swain, M. (1985). Communicative competence: Some roles of comprehensible input and output in its development. In S. Gass & C. Madden (Eds.), *Input in second language acquisition* (pp. 235–253). Rowley, MA: Newbury House.

Taylor, D. (1993). *From the child's point of view.* Portsmouth, NH: Heinemann.

Vygotsky, L. V. (1978). *Mind in society: The development of higher psychological processes.* Cambridge, MA: Harvard University Press.

Wittgenstein, L. (1957). *Philosophical investigations.* Oxford: Oxford University Press.

Zack, V. (1997). Nightmare issues: Children's responses to racism and genocide in literature. *The New Advocate: For Those Involved With Young People and Their Literature, 9,* 297–308.